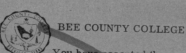

POLICE RIGHTS:
Civil Remedies for
Law Enforcement Officers

BY

CHARLES E. FRIEND

THE MICHIE COMPANY
Law Publishers
CHARLOTTESVILLE, VIRGINIA

TABLE OF CONTENTS

PART IV — PRACTICAL CONSIDERATIONS

TABLE OF CONTENTS

INTRODUCTION

This book was written to help police officers. All of them. Everywhere.

It is designed to acquaint individual police officers, police supervisors, police associations, and police legal advisors with the nature and extent of the civil remedies which are available to police personnel injured in any manner in the line of duty, and to provide a source of basic case authority and tactical guidance for attorneys representing police plaintiffs in tort actions.

The book's organization is simple. It begins with a general discussion which provides background information essential to an understanding of the present state of tort law as it applies to civil litigation by police officers. The second part deals with procedural and tactical matters related to the initiation of litigation. (The chapter dealing with the selection of defendants is of special — indeed, vital — importance to both the plaintiff officers and their attorneys.) The third part of the book examines in detail the specific types of civil suits which may be brought, and includes both a listing of the elements which must be proven in each form of action and a discussion of the application of that form of action to police plaintiff cases. Actual cases are cited wherever possible; where no decided case involving a police plaintiff has been found, cases supporting the general principle have been cited and, in some instances, arguments in favor of the extension of existing rules to cover police plaintiff cases have been suggested. The latter part of the book points out significant tactical aspects which have come to light in previous police plaintiff cases, and which should be considered by those contemplating such litigation.

This format should make it possible for the book to be useful in several ways. It should enable the individual officer to determine if a specific injury is compensable, and assist the officer in finding competent legal counsel to assist in making the decision whether or not to litigate and how to initiate that litigation. Police supervisors and police legal advisors should find it helpful when consulted by individual officers upon these same matters. Police departments and police officers' associations may wish to employ the book as a source of general information upon which to base decisions to encourage or discourage civil litigation by their members as a matter of organizational policy. Attorneys, whether they are police legal advisors, city attorneys, or private practitioners, should find the volume a useful source of case authority and general guidance in advising injured officers and in conducting litigation on behalf of the individual officers or their municipalities.

However, several words of warning are required.

1. This book is *not* intended to be a scholarly source of ultimate authority on the points covered. It is a basic reference manual, a primer, designed solely to introduce police officers, and others who have not previously been involved in police plaintiff cases, to the general principles of civil litigation by police.

2. While appellate case law has been cited wherever possible, the author does not represent that all existing cases have been cited or that the cases cited apply in a particular jurisdiction. There are, as yet, relatively few appealed cases involving police plaintiffs, and the appellate case law which exists is not indexed in the traditional legal research sources in a manner which makes it easily accessible to the researcher. This war is being fought in the trenches — in the municipal and superior trial courts. It may be years before a significant body of appellate case law is available to us for citation as authoritative precedent.

3. Because of the foregoing difficulty, some trial court decisions are cited here. While it is not usual to cite state trial court decisions in law reference books, it is done here because (a) appellate case law is often lacking on a particular point and (b) the trial court case may illustrate a

factual situation which is typical or may suggest a theory of recovery which other counsel may wish to try in their own jurisdictions. Trial court decisions are, of course, subject to appeal, and may be reversed by higher courts. Every effort has been made to avoid, or at least identify, such cases, but *no representation is made that any cited trial case has been approved by the higher courts of that jurisdiction.*

4. In addition, occasional references are made to cases in which the action has been *filed* but the results of the trial, if any, are not known. Like the decided trial court cases mentioned above, these undecided cases are mentioned *not as authority, but to illustrate factual situations and suggest possible theories of recovery,* which may or may not be accepted (yet) in any jurisdiction. In this field of the law, the stimulation of counsel's imagination is at least as important as the citation of appellate authority, and even a complaint which has been summarily dismissed by a lower court may suggest a new avenue of approach to another plaintiff in another jurisdiction.

5. This is a new area of the law and it is therefore developing rapidly. Cases establishing new rules and changing the old ones are being decided daily, and the law of a particular jurisdiction may differ markedly from holdings or general principles discussed in this book. Consequently, the user of this volume should take care to search the statutes and appellate decisions of his or her own jurisdiction; to examine local trial court decisions and attitudes; and to confer, if possible, with police associations and attorneys in the user's own geographical area to determine the current local law.

One other point should be noted. Police labor-management relations are beyond the scope of this book. With a very few exceptions, the principles discussed and the cases cited herein deal solely with tort litigation by police officers against persons outside of their own departmental hierarchies. Internal administrative matters, such as disciplinary procedures, pay and benefit negotiations, and hiring and promotion practices are not treated here. Such information is more properly covered in other volumes.

Within these limitations, however, I believe that this book will help to make law enforcement personnel aware of their rights and assist them in asserting those rights. I hope so, at least. I have watched with growing concern the increasingly poor treatment being accorded to law enforcement personnel in our society and in our legal system. As a lawyer, a law teacher, and a citizen I am disturbed by the trends that I observe. If this book helps — even just a little — it will have accomplished its purpose.

As I said at the beginning of this introduction, this book is dedicated to police officers. All of them. Everywhere.

CHARLES E. FRIEND

Campbell College, North Carolina

ACKNOWLEDGMENTS

The author wishes to express his sincere appreciation to the many individuals and organizations who assisted in the collection of information and material for this book.

Attorneys who provided information and advice based upon personal experience in police civil litigation include:

William E. Artz, Esquire
Arlington, Virginia

George J. Franscell, Esquire
Los Angeles, California

Jarrold Glazer, Esquire
Houston, Texas

Honorable Charles D. Haston, Judge
McMinnville, Tennessee

James Krueger, Esquire
Wailuku, Maui, Hawaii

John Lohmann, Esquire
Houston, Texas

Joseph E. Scuro, Jr., Assistant Attorney General
Legal Counsel, Ohio Highway Patrol
Columbus, Ohio

Jack B. Solerwitz, Esquire
Mineola, New York

Sincere thanks also to the following people for personal interviews or other assistance or materials:

Captain J. D. Bashinski
Union City Police Department
Union City, California

Robert C. Blount, Counsel
Division of Insurance Fraud
State of Florida
Tallahassee, Florida
formerly Special agent, Federal Bureau of Investigation

Harold Caldwell, Chief
Houston Police Department
Houston, Texas

William S. Phillips, Chief
Police Department
Abingdon, Virginia

Kenneth L. Risen, President
Los Angeles Police Protective League
Los Angeles, California

Frederic B. Weinstein, Regional Counsel
Commonwealth of Pennsylvania Department of Public
   Welfare
Philadelphia, Pennsylvania
formerly Assistant State's Attorney, Cook County
Chicago, Illinois

David Sheets, President
Houston Police Officers Association
Houston, Texas

My appreciation to these individuals for their courtesy in
responding to my various inquiries:

Jerome J. Blied, Field Staff Captain
Wisconsin State Patrol
Madison, Wisconsin

Richard J. Brzeczek, Executive Assistant to the
   Superintendent
Department of Police
Chicago, Illinois

W. T. Burke, Captain
Los Angeles Police Department
Los Angeles, California

Gerald L. Butler, Management Consultant
Board of Police Standards and Training
Salem, Oregon

Gareth H. Clift, Chief
Police Department
Cedar Rapids, Iowa

Thomas J. Deakin, Editor
FBI Law Enforcement Bulletin
Washington, D.C.

John A. Dienner, III, Assistant State's Attorney
Cook County
Chicago, Illinois

Harry J. Gaab, Chief
Lansdowne Police Department
Lansdowne, Pennsylvania

Robert C. Goodwin, Director
Tennessee Bureau of Criminal Identification
Nashville, Tennessee

John F. Hall, Supervisory Special Agent
Federal Bureau of Investigation
Los Angeles, California

Burtell M. Jefferson, Chief
Metropolitan Police Department
Washington, D.C.

Marjorie E. Lawson, Commander
Staff Services Section
California Highway Patrol
Sacramento, California

Edward Liggins, Sergeant
Police Department
San Francisco, California

Mark H. Neill
Assistant Legal Advisor
Board of Police Commissioners
St. Louis, Missouri

Lawrence C. Pritchard, Police Legal Advisor
Office of the Sheriff
Jacksonville, Florida

John S. San Diego, Sr., Chief
Police Department
Wailuku, Maui, Hawaii

Finally, my special thanks to

Frank Carrington, Executive Director
Americans for Effective Law Enforcement
Chicago, Illinois

Wayne W. Schmidt, Operating Director
Americans for Effective Law Enforcement
Chicago, Illinois

for making available to me information contained in the files
of Americans for Effective Law Enforcement, Inc., and for
providing me with introductions and other assistance.
Without their help, this book would not have been possible.

Part I
THE RIGHT TO SUE

Chapter 1

THE POLICE OFFICER'S RIGHT TO SUE

A. BACKGROUND

Law enforcement personnel always have been, and always will be, exposed to physical risk in the line of duty. There is an irreducible minimum of danger associated with the profession, and those who choose a career in law enforcement do so with the knowledge that the possibility of physical injury or death will always be present.[1]

In recent years, however, the incidence of line-of-duty injuries has been rising sharply. In particular, deliberate attacks upon officers are increasing at an alarming rate. Available statistics indicate that between 1965 and 1976 the total number of reported felonious assaults on city, county, and state police officers increased from 20,523 in 1965 to 49,079 in 1976. The number of officers killed by felons increased from 53 in 1965 to 107 in 1976, an increase of 239 percent; assaults which resulted in serious injuries rose from 6,836 in 1965 to 18,737 in 1976, an increase of 274 percent.[2]

Less widely publicized, but perhaps equally disturbing, is the remarkable rise in the number of *verbal* attacks on police officers in this country. While it is difficult to obtain exact figures, it is apparent that within the past few years American police officers (and police organizations) have been subjected to a rapidly escalating barrage of malicious and unfounded public accusations, including both false official complaints and defamatory statements published through the news media. While attacks of this nature cause no direct physical injury to the officer concerned, the damage to the officer's reputation and career, and the protracted legal

3

entanglements which may result from false charges, are often extremely detrimental to the mental, financial, and even physical health of the accused officers and their families.

In spite of the number of assaults, physical and verbal, which have been inflicted upon them, American law enforcement personnel have not generally attempted to utilize the civil courts as a source of redress for the wrongs done to them. While a certain number of civil suits have been brought over the years by police officers for job-related injuries, the number of actions filed is microscopic in comparison with the number of injuries being suffered. The civil remedy simply has not been the traditional response of the American police officer to line-of-duty injuries.

There are several clearly identifiable reasons for this nonuse of the civil courts, and an examination of these reasons is essential to anyone who may be called upon to advise an injured officer about civil remedies.[3]

1. *The Availability of Workmen's Compensation*

A major factor in the lack of use of the civil courts by injured officers has been the availability of workmen's compensation plans. Virtually every police officer in the country is covered through his or her department or agency by some form of plan whereby the officer is, in the event of injury, provided with medical care and protected against loss of income. These plans vary greatly in nature and scope of coverage, and many provide only minimal protection, but most officers who suffer a line-of-duty injury can expect to have direct medical expenses provided for, and to continue to receive salary and other benefits during at least some part of the period of disability.

Furthermore, this form of injury compensation is relatively easily obtained; such plans are generally administered directly through the departments themselves or their governmental bodies, and little or no action is normally required by the individual police officer to initiate a claim and to obtain whatever benefits are provided.[4] Furthermore, when medical bills are covered and no income is being lost, the officer may quite reasonably conclude that he has been satisfactorily compensated for the injury and feel no need to pursue the matter in a civil court.

2. *Lack of Awareness of the Availability of Civil Remedies*

While this is less of a factor today than it was a few years ago, there is some evidence that until relatively recently many police officers were not fully aware of the variety of civil remedies available or the extent of the compensation obtainable through a tort action. For example, while virtually every officer knows that a civil right of action exists for battery, until recently few would have been aware that the system provides them in some instances with a right of recovery for mental distress unaccompanied by any physical injury. Again, while most officers would be aware that a tort action can be brought to recover the direct expenses — such as medical bills — of an injury, some might be unaware of the availability of additional damages — *e.g.*, punitive damages, or an award for pain and suffering.[5]

This lack of knowledge has not been entirely confined to the officers involved. All too often, the attorneys consulted by these officers have failed to perceive possible avenues of recovery through lack of understanding of the lesser-known tort remedies.

Unfamiliarity of both officers and attorneys with the scope and extent of civil remedies has therefore played at least some small part in the nonuse of the civil court system by injured officers.

3. *Official and/or Public Discouragement of Civil Suits by Police*

Even if the injured officer is aware of the availability of civil remedies and is inclined to pursue them, the officer may be discouraged from doing so by official or public antipathy toward the use of civil remedies by police officers. Law enforcement agencies may, as a matter of policy, attempt to dissuade their personnel from filing civil suits based upon incidents arising in the line of duty. While this intra-departmental opposition may not be expressed openly, or even admitted publicly, it can be brought to the attention of the officer informally but with great force.[6]

In addition, the officer — and the officer's department — may be affected by opposition from segments of the public outside of the department itself. Civil rights groups, for example, tend to oppose the use of civil suits by police officers, and this opposition may result in pressure being brought to bear upon political leaders to discourage officers from resorting to civil actions.[7]

4. *The Difficulty of Obtaining Legal Representation*

The officer considering a civil suit may also encounter difficulty in finding an attorney who is willing to bring the action.

As noted above, many attorneys are not fully aware of the possibilities open to police plaintiffs in a civil court. In addition, the cost of good legal representation can be substantial, and the officer may not be willing to pay the fees required by the attorney, or the other costs associated with the civil litigation. In most localities, of course, plaintiffs' attorneys habitually accept cases on a contingent fee basis whereby the attorney will be paid an agreed percentage of the eventual recovery, if any. Unfortunately, for reasons described below, attorneys are often reluctant to accept

6

police plaintiff cases because they fear that even if a favorable verdict is obtained in court, they will be unable to collect the judgment, so that the net recovery — and the attorneys' contingent fee — will be nil.

5. *The Difficulty of Obtaining a Judgment*

An additional deterrent to civil action is the difficulty of obtaining a favorable judgment under the existing legal system. American tort law has, in some areas at least, developed a definite anti-police bias, which serves to block recoveries in many instances in which a wrong has unquestionably been done to the plaintiff officer. Thus, for example, the police officer may be confronted with complex legal defenses which deny to the officer the rights of the civilian citizen, or protect certain privileged defendants from the consequences of their wrongful acts.[8] Because of these discriminatory rules, certain types of civil actions may seem to the injured officer to present such difficulty as to become, if not impossible, at least unprofitable to pursue.

In addition, many officers feel that, regardless of the official rules of law involved, they will in practice be regarded unsympathetically by juries simply because they are police officers. (This apprehension may be groundless. See Damage Awards in Police Plaintiff Cases, Chapter 4.)

6. *The Difficulty of Collecting a Judgment Even If the Officer Wins the Case*

As noted in the discussion of the problems of obtaining legal representation, above, many attorneys shy away from police-plaintiff cases because they believe that, while the officer has a strong legal case and will obtain a favorable verdict in court, they will be unable to collect anything from the defendant after the judgment is rendered.

7

In certain types of cases, at least, this is a significant consideration, as, for example, in actions for battery. Unfortunately, those most likely to commit battery on a police officer are also those least likely to have substantial pecuniary assets with which to satisfy a judgment even if one is obtained. Consequently, both the officer and the attorney may consider it a waste of time to bring an action when it seems likely that any resulting judgment will be a hollow victory, with no money ever actually being collected from the indigent defendant.[9] In some instances, of course, the officer may wish to bring the suit as a matter of principle, or to obtain personal vindication; but these suits are relatively few, and in such instances the attorney will most probably require payment by the officer of a flat fee — in advance.

7. *The Attitude of the Individual Officer*

Although the difficulties discussed above are formidable, one of the most significant causes underlying the traditional lack of use of the civil courts by injured officers is the attitude of the officers themselves.

While individual officers are different, and therefore view the issues differently, certain common patterns of thought can be discerned. In the first place, as noted above, there is often an inherent distrust of the court system in general and of lawyers in particular. This leads to a feeling that there is no point in wasting time attempting to use a system which is basically hostile to the police officer, or which will place the officer's fortunes in the hands of lawyers, of which the police officer has not usually received a very favorable impression.

Secondly, there has quite commonly been a feeling among police officers that physical injury, or at least the risk of it, is just "part of the job," an occupational hazard which should be accepted without complaint. Most officers take pride in

8

being members of the law enforcement fraternity, but this is unfortunately often accompanied by a feeling of isolation from the civilian world. This strong sense of in-group identity in turn often leads to the feeling that it is not proper to complain to persons or institutions outside of the department when an injury is received. Fear of loss of face with (or even open ridicule by) brother officers may play a part here also, particularly where the injury is minor or of a strictly technical nature. In short, no one wants to appear to be a "crybaby."

This complex combination of pride and antipathy has historically discouraged many officers from filing civil suits; but, as will be noted later, this attitude seems to be changing rapidly today, especially where the case involves something other than the most minor physical or technical injury.

B. RECENT TRENDS IN CIVIL LITIGATION BY POLICE

Despite the difficulties described above, and the historical lack of use of civil remedies by law enforcement personnel, it appears that the trend is now toward increasing use of the civil courts by police plaintiffs. This trend (which is being referred to in some quarters as "blue lib") [10] has manifested itself in several ways.

First, there is a distinct increase in the number of cases reaching both the trial and appellate courts in which police officers are the complainants. Attorneys who specialize in representing police in civil litigation estimate that the number of actions being brought by officers as plaintiffs has at least doubled over the past two years; one source states that the "trend of police filing civil suits ... has sky-rocketed ...." [11]

9

Secondly, law enforcement-related publications are taking an increased interest in the subject; one such publication, *The Police Plaintiff*, now being produced by Americans for Effective Law Enforcement, Inc., of Evanston, Illinois, is devoted almost entirely to reporting and discussing cases in which a police officer has initiated civil proceedings.[12]

Even the new media have taken note of the development; articles have appeared, for example, in major city newspapers (*e.g.,* Washington Post, Feb. 5, 1978, at A6; Chicago Sun-Times, Feb. 12, 1978, at 14, and Akron Beacon-Journal, Feb. 12, 1978, at H1, H5) and in national magazines (*e.g.,* NEWSWEEK, March 6, 1978).

There are several factors which have contributed to this, and, again, an understanding of these is important to anyone involved in this area of the law.

1. *Increased Police Awareness of Civil Remedies*

The past few years have brought about changes in the law enforcement personnel themselves. Today's officers have a greater awareness of social issues in general and of their own rights in particular. This increased awareness is evident in the internal relationships between officers and their departments as well as in the officers' increased use of civil remedies against persons outside of their own agencies.[13]

2. *Increase in the Number of Injuries Being Suffered by Officers*

One very obvious cause of the increase in civil actions by police plaintiffs is the increase, discussed earlier in this chapter, in the number of injuries (physical and verbal) being inflicted annually upon officers. A greater number of injured officers means a greater number of tort claims by injured officers.

3. *Attitude of Officers Toward Certain Types of Injury*

Another factor, perhaps not quite so obvious, seems to be operating here also. It appears that while the average officer has been reluctant to bring a civil action for a physical assault (particularly where the actual injury is minor), a different attitude may be adopted when it is the officer's reputation which has been damaged. Although precise statistics are lacking, it appears that at present a clear majority of the civil actions being filed by police plaintiffs are for injuries related to reputation — libel, slander, etc. — rather than for injuries to the body. In fact, a study of the cases reported by *The Police Plaintiff* during the years 1976-1977 reveals that during that period, reported suits by law enforcement officers for defamation and false complaints exceeded reported suits for physical injuries *by a margin of more than two to one.* Clearly, many police officers do *not* regard unjustified verbal attacks upon their professional or personal reputations as being "just part of the job," and they are more ready to seek vindication in court for injuries of this type.

This attitude is of particular significance when one considers that, although both physical and verbal attacks upon police are increasing in frequency, the increase in verbal assaults seems to be proportionately greater. The emergence of the false complaint as a deliberate tactic to harass the police has caused a disproportionate increase in this type of attack. This trend, coupled with the difference in attitude being exhibited by officers toward verbal assaults, has undoubtedly accounted for much of the overall increase in police plaintiff suits.

4. *Increase in Litigation Against Police Officers*

In the past decade there has been an astronomical increase in litigation *against* police officers. In certain urban areas of the country, suing the police has become so commonplace that virtually every contact between police officer and civilian carries with it the threat of civil action against the individual officer, his supervisors, the department as a whole, and the city itself.[14] Police civil liability has become a topic of such importance that instruction in the subject is given in police training programs, independent organizations conduct regular workshops for police supervisors to prepare them to deal with the problem, and some departments — *e.g.*, Los Angeles — have even established special divisions or task forces to investigate civil complaints against them.

This increase in litigation *against* police has, in addition to making law enforcement personnel more aware of the civil side of our legal system, caused many officers to decide to stop being legal sitting ducks and to fight back against this "sue-the-cop" trend by utilizing the very same weapons that are being employed against them — lawyers and lawsuits, injunctions and money damages. The reasoning is simply that "if they can do it, why can't I?"

5. *Encouragement of Police Plaintiffs by Law Enforcement-Related Organizations*

Injured officers are now being openly encouraged by interested organizations to bring civil actions. Police associations have been particularly active in this regard. For example, police associations in New York, Texas, California, and Pennsylvania are reported to be openly and actively promoting the filing of civil actions by their members, or, in some cases, filing the actions themselves.[15] In some instances, this encouragement has been accompanied by a policy of making legal counsel available to officers interested in filing civil actions.[16]

This encouragement has not been confined to local police associations; national organizations such as Americans for

12

Effective Law Enforcement, Inc., and the International Conference of Police Associations have openly advocated the use of the civil courts by injured officers, and have provided interested officers with information and guidance toward that end.[17] In addition, some police departments have embraced "blue lib" as an official departmental policy.[18]

Each of these factors has contributed to the increase in litigation by police. The list is not necessarily complete, of course. There are other factors which operate in individual cases to encourage the bringing of civil suits. The point is that, whatever the reasons, the civil action is beyond doubt being increasingly used by American law enforcement officers. As Frank G. Carrington, Executive Director of Americans for Effective Law Enforcement, Inc., and author of several books and articles on victims' rights, puts it, "the police are deciding they don't have to be punching bags anymore." [19]

C. JUSTIFICATION FOR THE USE OF CIVIL ACTIONS BY LAW ENFORCEMENT PERSONNEL

This increasing willingness of law enforcement officers to institute civil suits for line-of-duty injuries is not being regarded with approval by all segments of our society. In fact, as will be noted subsequently, there is substantial opposition to the trend from such varied sources as civil rights groups, the news media, and even law enforcement agencies themselves.[20] A quick examination of the justifications being offered for the increased use of the civil suit by police plaintiffs is therefore necessary.

1. *Compensation of the Injured Officer*

The first and most obvious justification for the filing of any civil suit is the compensation of the injured plaintiff. This is the purpose of our system of tort law — to compensate those who have been injured by the wrongful acts of others. An elaborate system has been developed over a period of several centuries to accomplish that goal, and, with certain exceptions which will be noted in subsequent chapters,[21] the system does not distinguish between police officers and plaintiffs engaged in other occupations.

It is true, of course, that police officers are normally covered by some form of employee compensation plan applicable in cases of line-of-duty injuries. As previously noted, however, these plans normally provide only for direct medical expenses and continuation of income, and even these benefits may be subject to severe limitations as to duration or amount of coverage. In addition, they are applicable only in cases of illness or physical injury; injuries to reputation, for example, are beyond their scope.

By contrast, tort law provides remedies for injuries of all types, whether to the body, the mind, the reputation, the career, or just the technical rights of the officer. Further, even in a physical injury case, the damages obtainable in a civil action in a court of law are far broader in scope than those provided by even the most liberal workmen's compensation plan, and jury awards may reach figures unheard of in administrative compensation proceedings.

In addition, although the acceptance of workmen's compensation benefits usually precludes any further recovery from the employer, it does not normally prevent the bringing of a civil suit against a third party. Therefore, the officer may often collect benefits from the employing agency under an employees' compensation plan and, in addition, file a civil suit against any third person or persons who actually inflicted the injury. Thus, the officer may often be entitled to obtain compensation through both channels.[22]

Although sometimes condemned, this double compensation is perfectly lawful and is justifiable upon at least two grounds. First of all, it is entirely consistent with a

long-established tort doctrine known as the "collateral
source" rule, which holds that a wrongdoer is obligated to
pay for the full consequences of the wrong done, and is not
entitled to escape any portion of that obligation by virtue of
any benefits paid to the plaintiff by others.[23] Secondly, in the
event that an officer who has received benefits from an
employee compensation plan should recover a civil judgment
against a third party wrongdoer, the officer will, in many
instances at least, be required to reimburse the city or other
governmental agency for any benefits received from the
employee compensation plan. This relieves the burden on the
taxpayers, who would ultimately have borne the cost of the
injured officer's compensation under the employee benefit
plan; prevents the officer from receiving the "double
compensation" which some find so objectionable; and places
the financial burden where it belongs — on the wrongdoer
who caused the injury to begin with.[24]

2. *Prevention of Similar Attacks in the Future*

Advocates of the use of civil remedies by police personnel
have emphasized the potential value of such suits as a
deterrent to similar attacks on other officers. This reasoning
has been responsible in large part for the encouragement of
civil suits by police associations, which view this as a means
of countering the growing flood of physical and verbal
attacks and unfounded litigation against police officers. For
example, following the filing of a $2,000,000 lawsuit against
the Progressive Labor Party for injuries to nine policemen
during a "demonstration," Mr. Jerry D. Trent, a director of
the Los Angeles Police Protective League, was quoted as
saying that one of the reasons for the filing of the suit was
"to let groups like the Party know that 'unprovoked attacks
on our police officers simply will not be tolerated....'"[25]
Mr. George Franscell, attorney for the Los Angeles Police

15

Protective League, stated flatly that "what we are trying to do is make people understand they can't go along killing and maiming police and get away with it." [26] Similar statements have been made by officers or attorneys of the Dallas, Texas, Nassau and Suffolk County, N.Y., and Delaware County, Pennsylvania police associations.[27]

It is questionable whether the increased use of civil litigation by police officers or associations will have any effect upon "heat-of-passion" physical attacks on police officers by individuals. Such attacks are, of course, already punishable under criminal laws, whose sanctions are far more severe than mere money judgments. On the other hand, many advocates feel that the criminal law is now so heavily weighted in favor of the accused that it no longer represents a significant deterrent to any type of crime. If that is indeed the case, the certainty of civil action might be of some value in causing at least some potential assailants to have second thoughts, especially in the case of groups which advocate violence as a matter of policy.

The deterrent effect may be most noticeable in other types of cases, however. As previously noted, a major problem confronting law enforcement officials today is the increase in false complaints and unfounded civil litigation against officers and their agencies. Unlike most physical assaults, these verbal attacks are usually carefully premeditated, and are often launched only after legal counsel has been obtained by the complainant. The knowledge on the part of the prospective complainants (and their counsel) that civil penalties will be invoked for the filing of unfounded charges or legal actions may at least serve to discourage those persons — and their numbers appear to be substantial — who make complaints or file suits against the police with full knowledge that the charges have no basis in fact or law.

Much of the opposition to the use of civil suits by police officers centers about this latter point. Many feel that to encourage — indeed, even to permit at all — police officers to bring lawsuits against citizens will have a "chilling effect" upon people who have legitimate complaints against the police.

This argument does not impress advocates of increased use of the civil courts by police. They point out that, in the first place, those with legitimate complaints have no reason to fear civil action by the officer concerned, since only *unjustified* charges are wrongful under tort law, and that statistics indicate that the vast majority of official complaints and lawsuits filed against law enforcement officers are later proven to be unfounded and, in many instances, malicious.[28]

There is one additional and very persuasive argument made by those who favor the right of officers to bring civil action; they point out *that police officers are citizens too.* Why, it is argued, should the police officer who is shot, or stabbed, or beaten, or defamed have fewer civil rights than any other person? Police officers suffer pain, and bleed, and die, like everyone else. They leave behind them families who grieve and suffer financial hardship, just like everyone else. Why, then, should they be denied the rights to protection and compensation that our legal system accords to every other citizen?

This position has been summarized very nicely by Col. Adam G. Reiss, Superintendent of the Ohio State Highway Patrol:

> Law enforcement officers have the same rights as private citizens. Where any officers are injured civilly in the performance of their duties, they have the right, *and even a moral obligation,* to file suit.[29]

D. A SUMMARY OF THE PRESENT STATUS OF THE LAW

The overall status of civil litigation by police officers can be summarized as follows:

1. The present system of tort law provides a complete set of remedies for officers injured in the line of duty.

2. In some instances, recovery may be made difficult by technical defenses, but these difficulties are not normally of sufficient magnitude to justify abandoning the action entirely.

3. An increasing number of officers are making use of civil remedies, and substantial judgments are being recovered.

4. Officers interested in filing civil suits are receiving an increasing amount of support from police associations, law enforcement-related organizations, and the practicing bar.

5. Opposition to such suits exists in various segments of our society and will increase.

6. Police associations and other organizations and individuals can support the right of the police officer to utilize civil remedies by:

a. Increasing officer awareness of the availability of remedies.

b. Providing, or at least assisting the officer in obtaining, competent legal representation.

c. Supporting the development of statute and case law favorable to the police plaintiff.

This book is designed to facilitate these goals.

CHAPTER 1 — NOTES

1. That today's law enforcement officers are fully aware of the risks involved is amply demonstrated by recent studies of stress levels among law enforcement personnel. The effects of job-related stress upon the physical and mental well-being and the job performance of officers are now becoming a matter of serious concern to many police departments and other law enforcement-related organizations. *See,* for example, Stratton, *Police Stress — An Overview,* THE POLICE CHIEF, April 1978.

2. *See* FBI UNIFORM CRIME REPORTS, 1965, 1976. This increase is *not* due solely to the increase in the number of officers on duty. For example, in this same period the rate of reported assaults with injury rose from 3.6 per 100 officers in 1965 to 6.4 per 100 officers in 1976. In short, 6 officers out of every 100 on duty are now being killed or seriously injured each year. Note also that these are only the *reported* incidents; many minor attacks are not officially reported.

3. The terms "injured" or "injury" are used here and hereinafter to include both physical and verbal injuries, or, indeed, any unjustified act which is in any way damaging to the officer and is therefore actionable under the law.

4. This statement is intended only as a generalization. There are substantial variations in the amount of red tape involved in these plans, of course, and disputes over coverage can lead to lengthy administrative proceedings which are at least as protracted and aggravating as a civil trial.

5. *See* Ch. 4 *infra.*

6. *See* Ch. 10 *infra.*

7. *See* Ch. 10 *infra.*

8. *See* Ch. 10 *infra.*

9. This obstacle is not present in all types of cases, however, and attorneys who represent police plaintiffs are developing methods of overcoming the problem of the judgment-proof defendant. *See* Ch. 10 *infra.*

10. *See, e.g.,* Washington Post, Feb. 5, 1978, at A6.

11. THE BLUE LINE, Vol. 32, No. 9, at 3 (Aug. 1978) (publication of the Los Angeles Police Protective League).

12. *The Police Plaintiff* is published quarterly by Americans for Effective Law Enforcement, Inc., 960 State National Bank Plaza, Evanston, Illinois 60201. Articles on the subject have also appeared in the *FBI Law Enforcement Bulletin* and other periodicals.

13. There has been a substantial increase in the amount of litigation by officers against their own departments and municipalities over

disciplinary practices and other matters of an administrative nature. Such litigation is beyond the scope of this work, but the trends are probably related.

14. This trend has been apparent for some time. A survey of 1,604 law enforcement agencies conducted by the International Association of Chiefs of Police in the winter of 1973 disclosed that, on a projected national scale, between 1967 and 1971 — a period of only five years — the annual number of civil suits filed *against* police departments increased by almost 230%. IACP *Survey of Police Misconduct Litigation* (1973).

15. *See* THE POLICE PLAINTIFF, issues 76-1, at 7, 77-4, at 3, and 78-1, at 3. The Los Angeles Police Protective League has been particularly active, filing 50 civil suits in 1977 alone. THE BLUE LINE, Vol. 32, No. 9, at 3 (Aug. 1978).

16. *See* Ch. 2 *infra.*

17. Robert Gordon, Executive Director of the International Conference of Police Associations, reportedly told *The Washington Post* that "It used to be if a police officer was brought up on false charges . . . he would let it go if he was cleared. Now we tell them, 'Go after those people (the accusers) in civil suits.' " Washington Post, Feb. 5, 1978, at A6.

18. *E.g.,* Akron, Ohio. Akron Beacon-Journal, Feb. 12, 1978, at 45.

19. Washington Post, Feb. 5, 1978, at A6.

20. *See* Ch. 10 *infra.*

21. *See,* for example, Chs. 5 and 8 *infra.*

22. The officer may, however, then be required to repay the city any amounts received from the city in benefits. *See* the discussion of the "collateral source rule" in Ch. 4 *infra.* Furthermore, some statutes may force the officer to choose between accepting workmen's compensation benefits and suing the wrongdoer. *See* 106 A.L.R. 1040 (1937) for a full discussion.

23. *See* Ch. 4 *infra.*

24. *See* Ch. 3 *infra.*

25. THE POLICE PLAINTIFF, 78-1, at 4.

26. Washington Post, Feb. 5, 1978, at A6.

27. THE POLICE PLAINTIFF, 76-1, at 7; 77-4, at 3.

28. The 1973 IACP *Survey of Police Misconduct Litigation,* referred to in note 14 *supra,* revealed that of all known lawsuits filed against police during the survey period, only 24.1% were ever carried through to trial and, of these, 81.5% were won by the police officer.

29. As quoted in the Ravenna, Ohio, Record-Courier, Aug. 18, 1977 (emphasis added).

Part II
THE CIVIL SUIT

Chapter 2

INITIATING THE CIVIL ACTION

This chapter is designed primarily for the police officer who has not previously engaged in civil litigation as a plaintiff, or who is otherwise unfamiliar with the civil court system. It deals with certain preliminary matters essential to full understanding and utilization of tort remedies. Because it does deal with basic concepts, personnel who have previously engaged in civil litigation as plaintiffs may find that it covers matters already known to them, and attorneys will of course be well acquainted with the subjects discussed.

Nevertheless, an understanding of the fundamentals covered here will greatly enhance the possibility of a successful civil action by an injured officer, and the chapter is included for the benefit of those who wish to make certain that they have an adequate grasp of these first principles before proceeding further.

The chapter first examines the need for and method of obtaining legal counsel; the various types of civil action which may be available to the officer are then discussed in general terms; and, finally, the actual steps which need to be taken to initiate a civil action are briefly summarized.

Even those who have prior training or experience in tort law may find it profitable to examine the chapter, since the special importance in police cases of certain aspects of the system are pointed out in these introductory pages.

A. LEGAL REPRESENTATION

1. *The Need for Legal Representation*

Law enforcement personnel tend to have a low opinion of the legal profession. This is understandable, in view of the fact that most of the attorneys encountered by today's police officer are either criminal defense lawyers intent upon gaining acquittal for persons whom the officer has worked hard to place behind bars, often at great personal risk, or plaintiffs' lawyers engaged in suing the officer civilly for some alleged breach of a client's rights. This justifiable antipathy of police officers toward the bar has, as noted in Chapter 1, been one of the factors which has discouraged officers from attempting civil suits of their own.

This same suspicion and dislike, together with the question of the cost involved, may cause the officer who contemplates a civil suit to question whether it is necessary to employ legal counsel to bring the action, or if the officer's own familiarity with the legal system may be sufficient to make it possible for the officer to dispense with the services of legal counsel.

Although it is true that in certain courts, *e.g.*, small claims courts, lawyers are not required and may not even be permitted, in general it is essential that the officer who contemplates a civil action seek legal advice from some qualified attorney. As will be noted in the subsequent sections, this does not necessarily mean that the officer need incur expense in hiring a private practitioner, for other sources of advice may be available. Nevertheless, the failure to obtain competent legal advice prior to initiating any legal action — or deciding not to initiate such action — can be fatal to the officer's chances of success in a civil suit. Tort law is a complex field, and the rules which apply to cases involving police plaintiffs are sometimes particularly complex. Only a competent attorney familiar with the applicable law will be in a position to discuss the case with the officer and to determine:

a. Whether the officer has a right of action at all;

b. If there is a right of action, what form the action should take;

c. Whether, under the facts, the chances of obtaining a recovery justify the bringing of the action, and;

24

d. What amount the officer might reasonably expect to recover for the injury involved if the action is successful.

Failure to seek legal advice before bringing suit may even result in the officer being held liable for malicious prosecution, etc. (See Chapters 7 and 10.)

In most instances, therefore, legal representation is desirable and should be obtained if it is possible to do so.

2. *Selection of an Attorney*

The problem of selecting an attorney to represent the injured officer in a civil case is complicated by the fact that the attorneys with whom officers are most likely to be familiar are not necessarily those best suited for the bringing of a civil action. Prosecuting attorneys are usually barred from representing officers in civil suits, and the criminal defense lawyers that the officer sees most frequently in court often confine themselves to the practice of criminal law and are therefore unfamiliar with tort actions. While criminal trial law and civil trial law bear many similarities and require similar talents, the differences in theory and tactics are nevertheless significant, and it is therefore normally preferable to obtain counsel who is more familiar with the civil system.[1] In general, then, the officer should attempt to obtain the services of an attorney who is experienced in the conduct of civil trials.

It should also be noted that civil trial lawyers often specialize in representing either plaintiffs or defendants. Obviously, the officer should ascertain whether the attorney under consideration is experienced in bringing lawsuits as well as in defending them.[2]

Clearly, the ideal attorney for the officer is one who has had previous experience in *representing police plaintiffs.* As noted elsewhere, police plaintiff cases involve certain

25

problems not encountered in actions by other types of plaintiffs, and the attorney who has already engaged in this type of litigation will usually be best equipped to advise the officer properly and to conduct the officer's suit to the best effect.

It appears that most urban areas now have one or more attorneys who have specialized in, or at least handled a number of, civil cases involving police officers. Typically, these attorneys will more often have represented the officers as defendants than as plaintiffs (as noted earlier, the amount of civil litigation *against* police officers exceeds the amount of civil litigation *by* police officers); nevertheless, an attorney with this background is often the best possible choice for the injured police officer seeking representation as a plaintiff. Not only are such attorneys skilled in the theory, strategy, and tactics of tort law, but also they are generally more sympathetic to police officers and understand the officer's problems better than the average lawyer.[3]

In small towns or rural areas, it may be difficult to find an attorney experienced in representing police plaintiffs, or plaintiffs generally, or even one who specializes in civil law. In such areas, specialization is often not possible, and general practitioners are the rule rather than the exception. In that event, the officer should look for the attorney in the area who is most experienced in *trial law*. The common denominators present in both civil and criminal litigation make the lawyer who makes his living in the courtroom preferable, in most instances, to even the most erudite "office lawyer."[4]

Naturally, any attorney chosen should be competent. Experience is not always synonymous with capability. Skill is the ultimate criterion in selecting an attorney, regardless of background.

Finally, there is of course the problem of cost. Lawyers differ greatly in their charges, and the officer must locate counsel who is flexible enough in fee matters to make it possible for the officer to afford to bring the action. (The fee problem is discussed further, below.)

The officer seeking legal counsel has, in addition to personal knowledge, several possible sources of information, including:

a. The Officer's Police Association or Similar Organizations. Police associations usually have their own lawyers, who often also handle cases for officers; if not, the association is usually able to provide the officer with a list of attorneys in the area who are known to take police civil cases.

b. Fellow Officers. Other officers who have been represented by local attorneys in civil cases are an excellent source of reference. In addition to identifying attorneys who are experienced in police civil cases, officers who have actually been represented by an attorney can evaluate the performance of that attorney from firsthand knowledge, and advise the prospective plaintiff as to whether the attorney in question is competent, sympathetic, aggressive, charges fairly, etc.

c. City Attorneys' or District Attorneys' Offices. Even though attorneys employed by the city or state as prosecutors or legal advisors for the governmental body may not be able to represent the officer, they are usually aware of the identity and capabilities of private practitioners in the local area who might be suitable counsel for the injured officer.

d. Local Bar Referral Services. Many areas now have referral services which can be consulted by any citizen in need of legal assistance. These referral services are less well suited to the needs of the injured police officer than the other sources of information discussed above, but may be consulted as a last resort.

Of course, the individual officer may have personal knowledge of a suitable attorney, or may know a particular attorney who, though not qualified to handle the case, may be able to refer the officer on to someone else. The officer should bear in mind, however, that close personal acquaintance — or even friendship or kinship — to an attorney does not alone make that attorney the ideal choice to handle the officer's case. Again, the foremost criterion should be *demonstrated competence at handling trial work for police plaintiffs.* While the absence of this quality *may* be compensated for by other factors — such as personal friendship — choosing an attorney by other critieria is a calculated risk and should not be done lightly.

The Acknowledgments at the beginning of this book contain a list of persons who assisted the author in the preparation of this book. Some of them are attorneys actively engaged in representing police officers in civil litigation; others are officials of police associations, etc. Officers without other sources of information may find that one or more of these people will be able to assist the officer in locating someone who is able to represent the officer in a particular case.

3. *Legal Fees and Costs*

The costs of litigation can be substantial, and this can and does deter many officers from filing suit. These costs can be broken down into three main categories:

    a. Attorneys' fees.
    b. Court costs.
    c. Other expenses of litigation.

Court costs include fees for filing the action and other costs charged by the court to defray the court's own costs.

Expenses of litigation might include such matters as expert witness fees (*e.g.,* the cost of hiring a doctor to examine the officer and testify as to the extent of the injury) and the cost of taking depositions.

Normally, however, the major problem is the attorney's fee, which generally exceeds all other costs, and the officer has several possible alternatives.

a. Counsel Provided Without Charge to the Officer Through a Professional or Governmental Organization.

In some instances, the officer may be able to obtain representation without cost through some private organization or through the governmental body by which he or she is employed. The former is more likely than the latter. For example:

(1) Police associations, particularly those which are actively encouraging officers to file civil actions, may be able to provide legal representation without cost to the officer. This may be done, for example, by having the association's own attorney act as the injured officer's lawyer,[5] or by having the case brought in the name of the association itself, for the benefit of the injured officer.[6] At least one police association has established a "Legal Rights Fund" to provide financial backing for suits by its members.[7] Unfortunately, the average association will not be able to bear the cost of numerous suits by individual officers, and, on the other hand, will be forced to be selective in deciding just which suits will be brought by the association itself. Consequently, this method of obtaining legal counsel is not open to many officers.

(2) Many urban areas have city attorneys' offices which work closely with the police department in civil suits *against* police officers. Such suits are often defended by city attorneys on behalf of the city and/or

29

the individual officer. Unfortunately again, city and state's attorneys are usually precluded by ethical considerations, policy, administrative regulations, court decisions, or statutes or ordinances from representing individual officers as *plaintiffs*.[8] (It should be kept in mind, however, that city or state attorneys may be able to file counterclaims in such actions, thereby in effect assuming a supplementary role as counsel for the plaintiff on the counterclaim.[9])

Police legal advisors are also usually prohibited from acting on behalf of police plaintiffs.

Nevertheless, city and state's attorneys and police legal advisors are often consulted by officers as informal sources of preliminary information, *e.g.*, about other attorneys (see Selection of an Attorney, above). Where this is done, the officer should keep in mind that the city attorney or p.l.a. (1) may not be qualified to determine whether there is or is not a possible tort cause of action under the facts and (2) may be under departmental or municipal pressure to discourage civil actions by officers.

b. Counsel Fees Paid by the Officer.

All too often, there is no organizational source of formal legal representation, and fee arrangements must be made by the individual officer. Here there are three basic possibilities: the flat fee, the hourly fee, and the contingent fee.

(1) *Flat Fee.*

The attorney may simply wish to set a fixed fee prior to beginning litigation. This is often true with cases in which the dollar amount sued for is small, *e.g.*, where injuries are minor or where the suit is being brought purely as a matter of principle or to vindicate the officer's own behavior. The attorney may request that the entire fee be paid in advance, or may be willing to allow the officer to delay payment of all or part of the fee until some later date or dates. This method has the virtue of enabling the officer to determine in advance exactly what the fee will be, but, of course, the officer will be responsible for payment regardless of the outcome of the case.

(2) *Hourly Fee.*

Some attorneys prefer not to charge a fixed fee in advance, but to charge the client on a per hour basis for the time actually expended in pursuing the case. This method may be advantageous to the officer if the case proves to be a simple one, or is settled quickly, but it does have the disadvantage of uncertainty — the officer does not know in advance what the attorney's fees may turn out to be, and at $50 per hour and up, a long and complicated case can become expensive. And, again, the officer will be responsible for payment of the fee regardless of the outcome of the case.

(3) *Contingent Fee.*

A common practice among plaintiffs' lawyers is to set no flat or hourly fee, but to base the fee upon a percentage of any eventual recovery. For example, the attorney may ask that the fee be 25 percent of any amount recovered from the defendant by means of a settlement before trial, $33^{1}/_{3}$ percent if the case goes to trial, and 40 percent if the trial decision is appealed.

The contingent fee system has many critics, but it does at least enable those lacking the financial ability to pay a fixed fee in advance to obtain legal representation and assert their legal rights in court. Most officers will find this fee arrangement superficially attractive, because it appears to provide the officer with legal counsel at no out-of-pocket cost. One possible pitfall should be noted, however: many lawyers are reluctant to undertake cases for injured police officers on a contingent basis because they feel that,

31

although the officer has a good chance of obtaining a judgment, there is little chance of ever satisfying that judgment from the empty pocket of an impecunious defendant. The contingent fee is usually based on *the amount actually obtained from the defendant, not upon the amount of the judgment.* Consequently, the attorney may attempt to discourage the officer from pursuing what is otherwise a good cause of action, if the officer insists upon a contingent fee agreement. (In Chapter 10, the problem of enforcement of judgments is discussed in detail, and suggestions are made for increasing the chances of obtaining satisfaction of any judgment rendered. The alternatives suggested in that discussion may make the contingent fee arrangement more attractive to attorneys in many instances where they are now reluctant to proceed on a contingent fee basis.)

Under any of these fee arrangements, the officer will remain responsible for the other costs of litigation, and, even under a contingent fee arrangement, will be required to pay these regardless of the outcome of the case. (The court may, however, if the plaintiff officer is successful in obtaining a judgment, require the defendant to pay the plaintiff's court costs.)

c. Counsel Fees Paid by Defendant.

Generally speaking, tort law does not permit attorneys' fees to be awarded to the plaintiff.[10] There are, however, some indications that this position is changing, and in certain instances *the officer may be able to recover attorneys' fees from the defendant* if the officer is successful in proving his or her case.

In some instances, for example, a statute may require the payment of one party's attorneys' fees by the other party. States frequently have legislation providing that the court may order the losing party to pay the winning party's attorneys' fees, or some part of them.[11] In addition, the

32

federal Civil Rights Act now includes a provision for payment by the loser of the prevailing party's attorneys' fees.[12]

In many instances punitive damages can be recovered from the defendant, and this is recognized as one means of obtaining indirectly from the defendant enough money to cover the attorneys' fees. (Punitive damages are discussed in Chapter 4.)

Counsel should of course attempt to obtain an award of attorneys' fees by the court regardless of the nature of the fee agreement with the plaintiff officer.

B. TYPES OF CIVIL ACTION

In considering the various types of civil action which may be available to the police officer for injuries suffered in the line of duty, two points should be kept in mind:

(1) There are several ways of categorizing civil actions, and these different methods of categorization overlap, so that any one specific tort action may be classified several different ways, or indeed may be difficult to categorize at all because the action involves several different elements.

(2) In practice, exact categorization is usually unnecessary, because (a) the specific forms of action are generally long established and fully recognized in all jurisdictions, and (b) under modern pleading rules, it may be unnecessary to label your complaint with any specific name, as long as it is made clear in the pleadings that a wrong occurred and needs redress. Consequently, the following categorizations are *for instructional purposes only,* and the prospective plaintiff need not be overly concerned if the plaintiff's particular problem does not seem to fit readily into any particular pigeonhole.

1. *Classification by Nature of the Relationship Between the Parties: Tort and Contract*

A tort is a wrong done by one individual to another independent of the existence of any contract agreement between the parties. It is the violation of a general duty, imposed upon all persons by the law, not to injure one another without justification.[13] Unlike contract actions, therefore, in the tort action the plaintiff and defendant usually have not made any prior agreement between themselves and indeed may never have had any contact whatsoever with one another prior to the moment of the commission of the tort.

In contract actions, by contrast, there is normally some prior transaction or agreement between the parties which has been violated by one of them, and it is this breach of an express agreement which is the cause of the suit. Under certain circumstances, contract obligations may arise where there is no express agreement or actual transaction between the parties,[14] but the bulk of contract actions involve some express understanding, written or oral, between individuals, or some prior transaction in which although there is no express agreement, the conduct of the parties or some rule of law creates enforceable obligations. An example of the latter type of action which may be of interest to police officers is the action for "breach of warranty," in which an officer injured by a defective piece of equipment may have a right of action based upon an express *or implied* guarantee (warranty) from the seller that the product is safe and will do what it is supposed to do.[15]

Most actions involving police plaintiff are tort actions (with the exception of employment and disciplinary matters which are beyond the scope of this book); consequently, the remainder of this discussion is devoted to tort remedies.

34

2. Classification by Nature of the Defendant's Wrongdoing: Intentional Torts, Negligence, and Strict Liability

Tort actions are commonly classified as intentional, meaning roughly that the defendant did it on purpose, or negligent, meaning that the defendant intended no harm but was merely careless. An example of an intentional tort would be battery; a common basis for negligence actions is the motor vehicle accident.[16]

In some jurisdictions, defendants will also be held liable for certain injurious acts even though the act was done without intent to cause harm and with all due care; this is referred to as "strict liability." Relatively few police plaintiff actions are brought on a strict liability theory, although the concept is becoming important in products liability actions.[17]

It should be added that many torts do not fit neatly into any one of these classes; many tort actions involve elements of both intent and negligence and may, depending upon the facts, be maintained on either theory, with strict liability as an occasional third possibility.

3. Classification by Type of Injury: Personal Injury, Property Damage, Etc.

Tort actions, whether intentional, negligent, or based upon strict liability, may also be classified according to the type of injury which results to the plaintiff. For example, some actions involve physical injury to the person (*e.g.,* when a police officer is beaten or struck by an automobile); these cases are referred to as "personal injury actions." If death results, the action is called "wrongful death," and is usually governed by a state statute rather than by common-law principles. Actions may also be brought where the defendant has inflicted no *physical* injury at all but has negligently or intentionally caused the plaintiff serious *mental* anguish;

35

this branch of tort law is called "infliction of mental distress." [18]

If the officer's property has been damaged, or if damage has been done by the defendant to property belonging to the department for which the officer is responsible, an action may be maintained for property damage alone. Such actions would include "trespass to chattels" or "conversion" if personal property were damaged, or, if real property such as land or a house were involved, "trespass to land" might be the appropriate remedy.[19] The foregoing are all intentional torts; alternatively, a negligence action might be appropriate.

The law also provides a remedy for injuries to a person's reputation; false derogatory statements about someone are actionable as "libel" or "slander." [20]

In addition, there are many instances where no tangible injury to body, mind, property, or reputation has necessarily occurred, but the law, for policy reasons, requires that the defendant be held civilly liable, at least for nominal damages.[21] This category includes such varied types of actions as "false arrest" and "invasion of privacy." [22]

The examples given in each instance are, of course, only a few of the specific tort actions that may fit into that particular category; and, as noted, any specific tort may fit into several of these general categories, or may not fit into any of them at all.

The selection of the type of action which fits the fact of the particular case is, of course, one of the primary responsibilities of the plaintiff's lawyer. (See below.)

C. PROCEDURE FOR INITIATION OF A CIVIL ACTION

Police officers are normally thoroughly familiar with the procedure for initiation of criminal proceedings, but the steps which must be taken to institute a civil suit are substantially different and may therefore be unfamiliar.

1. *Employing an Attorney*

The first step, as noted earlier, is usually to retain a competent attorney. The attorney's role will then be to discuss the case fully with the officer and to help the officer to make several very important decisions, as follows:

a. What Type of Action Should Be Filed?

The type of action to be instituted must be decided. For example, should the claim be made as one for an intentional tort, such as battery, or would it be better to characterize the defendant's behavior as negligence? Or should both claims be made? This decision can be critical to the chances of obtaining a judgment. (See Chapter 11.)

b. What Person or Persons Should Be Named as Defendants?

More than one person may be liable. If so, should all be sued? If not, which one or ones should be named in the suit? Upon this answer may depend the chances of *collecting* a judgment even if one is rendered. The problem is discussed at length in Chapter 3.

c. What Should the Plaintiff Ask for?

What relief should be asked for in the suit? If money damages are to be sought, what amount should be claimed? Should any other remedy — *e.g.,* injunction — be sought? The forms of relief available are discussed in Chapter 4.

d. In What Court Should the Action Be Brought?

In tort actions, the plaintiff usually has a choice of courts in which to bring the action. For example, if the amount claimed is small, it may be advisable — or even necessary — to bring the suit in a lower court, such as a district or

37

municipal court; if the amount claimed is larger, a higher court, usually called a circuit or superior court, may or must be selected. Regardless of the amount involved, the plaintiff usually has a choice of courts, for *tort action typically may be brought in more than one jurisdiction* — e.g., in the jurisdiction where the defendant lives, or in the jurisdiction where the tort was committed, if different from the defendant's place of residence.

Other tactical decisions such as whether to take depositions, ask for trial by jury, etc., will, of course, have to be made with the help of the attorney prior to the actual filing of the suit; the foregoing are merely examples.

2. *Filing the Action*

The second step is usually the actual commencement of the court action. This is normally done by filing a "complaint" (called in some jurisdictions a "motion for judgment") in the selected court. This document sets forth at length the facts of the case, states the legal grounds upon which the plaintiff feels that a recovery is justified, and requests relief, *e.g.,* money damages in a certain amount.[23]

3. *Serving the Complaint*

The complaint is then served upon the defendant(s), usually by an officer such as a deputy sheriff, city sergeant, process server, etc.

4. *Defendant's Response*

The defendant then has a specified number of days to respond to the complaint with defensive pleadings or motions. If the defendant fails to act within this allotted time period, defendant is normally considered to be "in default," and a judgment may be rendered against the defendant by the court without a trial. These "default judgments" are often later set aside by the court for various reasons, but are otherwise perfectly valid and enforceable, and the plaintiff may proceed immediately to attempt to collect from the defendant the amount awarded to the plaintiff by the court.

5. *Settlement or Abandonment of the Action*

If the defendant should — as is normally the case — respond within the time period allotted, the case will usually proceed to trial unless the defendant and the plaintiff agree to settle the case out of court or the plaintiff decides to abandon the action. The out-of-court settlement is fairly common, but a plaintiff officer who has obtained competent legal advice prior to instituting the suit will not normally abandon the action without some compensation being paid, unless new facts come to light which weaken the officer's case or other circumstances (such as departmental or political pressure) arise which make it undesirable to pursue the action.

6. *Trial*

The trial itself follows the same general pattern as a criminal trial. The procedural and evidentiary rules are for the most part the same, with certain significant exceptions. Three of these major differences between civil and criminal trials are:

(a) Whereas in a criminal trial the state must prove the accused guilty beyond a reasonable doubt, in a civil case the plaintiff need establish the defendant's fault only by a "preponderance of the evidence," a lighter burden of proof.

(b) Whereas in a criminal trial the accused cannot be forced to take the witness stand, in a civil trial the plaintiff may, if desirable, call the defendant to the stand and elicit answers from the defendant about the defendant's behavior.[24]

(c) Whereas in a criminal trial, the accused's own statements may often not be used against him by the prosecution because of the strictures of the *Miranda* rule, etc., in civil trials virtually *any* statement made by the defendant may be used against him or her by the plaintiff without prior recourse to complicated warnings about self-incrimination or right to counsel. (In civil trials the defendant's statements are referred to not as "confessions" but as "party admissions" or "admissions against interest.")

Obviously, the foregoing outline of procedure is very brief and very general. Actual procedures may vary widely in different jurisdictions. Here again, it is the obligation and function of the attorney to explain to the plaintiff officer what procedure is required and to execute the necessary steps to institute the action mutually decided upon.

We will now turn to consideration of the vital matter of determining what persons shall be named as parties to the action.

CHAPTER 2 — NOTES

1. Many attorneys, of course, handle both criminal and civil trials, and are therefore skilled in both areas.

2. Again, many lawyers are experienced in both.

3. Many such attorneys are themselves ex-officers, or have acted in some official capacity (*e.g.,* prosecutor or city attorney) which has made them knowledgeable about and sympathetic toward law enforcement personnel.

4. Another alternative might be to go outside the local area to the nearest large city to obtain the services of a "specialist" of the type already described. The officer must balance the advantage of having an "outside" specialist against the advantage enjoyed by the local attorney of greater familiarity with the courts and juries in the local area. In some communities, this local expertise can be of great value, and may outweigh the experience of an outsider. The choice is often a difficult one for the officer to make.

5. Some police associations in the New York City area are reportedly providing legal services free of charge to officer-plaintiffs. THE POLICE PLAINTIFF, 76-1, at 7.

6. *See, e.g.,* THE POLICE PLAINTIFF, 78-1, at 7-8.

7. Fraternal Order of Police Lodge 27, Delaware County, Pennsylvania, as reported in THE POLICE PLAINTIFF, 77-4, at 3.

8. *See, e.g.,* People *ex rel.* Carey v. Lincoln Towing Serv., Inc., 40 Ill. App. 3d 126, 351 N.E.2d 342 (1976) (state's attorney cannot represent one private citizen against another).

9. As occurred in the case of Geisler v. Bianco, 74-C-2671 (N.D. Ill. 1976), in which an assistant state's attorney representing the defendant police officer counterclaimed against the plaintiff and obtained an award of $2,500 for the officer. As to counterclaims generally, *see* Ch. 11 *infra.*

10. *See* Ch. 4 *infra.*

11. *See, e.g.,* Dowden v. Liberty Mut. Ins. Co., 346 So.2d 1311 (La. App. 1977), in which an injured officer sued the city's workmen's compensation insurance carrier for refusing to pay the officer's claim, and the court ordered the insurance company to pay not only the original claim, but also the attorney's fees incurred by the officer in pursuing the claim, in accordance with Louisiana Revised Statutes 22:658. This is a common provision in workmen's compensation statutes. Other types of statutes may provide for payment of attorneys' fees by the loser. Unfortunately, these statutes often provide for payment of only miniscule amounts. *See, e.g.,* VA. CODE § 14.1-196 ($50.00 in cases brought before the Supreme Court of Virginia).

12. 42 U.S.C. § 1988, as amended by Pub. L. No. 94-559 § 2 (1976).

13. For expansion of this and other terms discussed here, the reader is referred to BLACK'S LAW DICTIONARY, BALLANTINE'S LAW DICTIONARY, or similar publications.

14. So-called "quasi-contract" actions are possible where the parties have never had prior dealings, but these will not be discussed here.

15. *See* Ch. 5 *infra.*

16. *See* Ch. 5 *infra.*

17. *See* Ch. 5 *infra.*

18. *See* Ch. 6 *infra.*

19. *See* Ch. 9 *infra.*

20. *See* Ch. 8 *infra.*

21. *See* Ch. 4 *infra.*

22. *See* Chs. 7, 9 *infra.*

23. In some lower courts, the action may be commenced by obtaining what is usually called a "civil warrant." This document, normally obtained from a lower court judge, court clerk, magistrate, or justice of the peace, takes the place of the complaint or motion for judgment in some jurisdictions. This "civil warrant" differs from an arrest warrant in that no affidavits or probable cause need be shown; it is merely requested and issued — for a fee.

24. It should be added that, while it is *permissible* to do this, it may not be *wise,* since the defendant will be, at best, a hostile and evasive witness when called by the plaintiff. This is a tactical decision for plaintiff's counsel to make, and it is not often done.

Chapter 3

PARTIES TO THE ACTION

Two questions will immediately confront any officer (or officer's attorney) planning a civil suit for line-of-duty injuries. These are:

1. Who can sue?
2. Who can be sued?

At first glance, these questions may seem unnecessary or even frivolous, since the person who is injured is normally the plaintiff, and the person who committed the act which caused the injury is normally the defendant. Nevertheless, the problem is not quite that simple. In the first place, *parties other than the person actually injured may have a right of recovery against the wrongdoer.* These may include, for example, the families of the injured officers, or the municipalities which employ the officers. Failure to recognize the rights of these additional persons or agencies, or failure to exercise their rights in a proper case, is a denial of those rights and therefore an injustice. *Officers and their counsel should examine the facts carefully to determine whether additional rights of action exist in persons or entities other than the individual officer.*

Secondly, *there are many instances in which some person, group, organization, etc., other than the immediate wrongdoer is legally responsible for the conduct of the wrongdoer and may be obligated to compensate the plaintiff for the wrongdoing.* Failure to recognize the possibility of joining additional defendants in the action will of course result in these persons escaping responsibility for their own obligations and, of greater practical importance to the plaintiff, may result in the plaintiff being unable to obtain compensation; the actual wrongdoer may be unable to satisfy a judgment, whereas the legally responsible but unsued person or organization may have substantial financial assets which could have been used to compensate the officer if that other person or organization had been named as a defendant in the suit. Here again, therefore, *officer and counsel should study the case carefully to ascertain whether additional defendants may be brought into the case and may be called upon to satisfy a judgment when one is obtained.*

A. PLAINTIFFS—WHO CAN SUE?

1. *The Injured Officer*

In virtually every case, the individual officer who has been the victim of a physical or verbal attack or who has been otherwise wronged by the defendant(s) has, initially at least, the right to bring the action. Normally, then, the individual officer will be the plaintiff. In most jurisdictions, where more than one person has been injured in the same incident the individual actions of these several plaintiffs may be consolidated into one action, although the courts usually have discretion to order separate trials.[1] Whether consolidated or not, these are individual actions, and they should not be confused with class actions, discussed below.

Under certain circumstances, it may be necessary for the action to be brought by someone else on behalf of the officer or in his place. Thus, for example, if the officer has been killed, the action will be brought as a wrongful death action by the person or persons designated in the governing statute, for the benefit of the family of the deceased victim;[2] or, if the officer, although still alive, is now physically or mentally incompetent to act in his own behalf, a guardian may be appointed by the court to act as plaintiff in behalf of the officer;[3] or the injured officer, though alive and competent, may, by accepting benefits through an employer's compensation plan, be required to assign his own right to sue to the agency or company paying the benefits — a process known as subrogation.[4]

44

Barring one of these circumstances, however, the injured officer has and retains the right to institute the legal action in his own behalf.

2. *The Family of the Injured Officer*

The family of an officer injured or killed in the line of duty often suffers great hardship. Fortunately, the law provides that the family members, especially the spouse and children, of the injured or deceased person have rights of action of their own against the wrongdoer, and these rights are separate from and in addition to any rights of the injured officer.[5]

a. Actions by the Family for Wrongful Death of the Officer.

As noted above, the family of an officer killed in the line of duty (or otherwise, for that matter) normally has a right to bring suit against the person responsible for the death. This right is considered in most states to belong to the surviving family members, rather than to the officer, and any recovery obtained will, after payment of certain of the officer's expenses, go to the family (normally the spouse and/or children, if any). Wrongful death is discussed in detail in Chapter 5.

b. Actions by the Family for Physical Injury of the Officer.

Members of the family may also have a separate right of action where the officer has suffered physical injury but has survived. Most of these cases fall into two general categories: (1) actions by the officer's spouse and (2) actions by the officer's children, parents, or other relatives.

(1) *Actions by the Injured Officer's Spouse.*

The common law from very early times permitted a husband whose wife had been injured to recover from the person who caused the injury for loss of "consortium" of the

45

wife, meaning basically that he had been deprived of her services and companionship. In recent times, this same right of recovery has been extended to the wife in the event of injury to the husband, so that today the spouse — whether husband or wife — of the injured officer will, in many jurisdictions, have a separate cause of action against the person who caused the injury to the officer. In one such case, for example, the court upheld a judgment of $10,000 in favor of the wife of a beaten officer, saying:

> Damages for loss of consortium represent compensation due to a wife who has been deprived of rights to which she is entitled by virtue of the marriage relationship, namely, her husband's affection, companionship, comfort, assistance, and particularly his conjugal society. The evidence ... shows that the last months of her marriage were unhappy due to the intentional injury inflicted on her husband by the defendants.[6]

(2) *Actions by the Injured Officer's Children, Parents, or Other Relatives.*

There has been relatively little recognition by the courts of a child's right to sue for injury to a parent. It is apparently assumed that the spouse's recovery for loss of the services and society of the injured person would also benefit the child of the marriage. Nevertheless, action by the child of an injured officer-parent may be possible, and counsel should investigate the law of the particular jurisdiction.

An action by the *parent* for the loss of the *child's* services has long been recognized at common law, but since this right normally terminates when the child becomes "emancipated" (*i.e.,* grows up and gets a job), it will probably seldom be possible for the parents of an injured officer to bring action in their own right for injury to the officer not resulting in death.[7] Similarly, other more distant relatives seldom if ever will have a right of action of their own for injuries to the officer-relative. Nevertheless, local law should be examined to determine if there is any such right in parents or other kin in that particular jurisdiction.

c. Actions for Defamation.

Although in the normal case libelous or slanderous statements about an officer affect solely the officer's own reputation, counsel should be alert to the possibility that the reputation of a family member — such as a spouse or child — has been impugned as well. Although family members are seldom mentioned expressly in verbal attacks on officers, derogatory statements about the officer may affect the reputation of the family member by implication, thereby giving the family member a separate right of action.

d. Threats, Harassment, and Mental Distress.

As officers who have become the target of campaigns of harassment know, family members are often directly affected by such attacks. For example, the officer's wife may receive obscene or threatening telephone calls, or a family pet may be poisoned. Whenever the family suffers directly from such actions, the family members will normally have the same right of action that would accrue to the officer, even if the action of the perpetrators was directed primarily at the officer. The principles under which the family members may recover in such cases are discussed in the chapter dealing with those specific problems.[8]

e. Invasion of Privacy.

The police officer's right of action for invasion of privacy is not yet well developed; there are few known cases, and indeed the entire area of invasion of privacy is in a state of transition and may not be fully recognized in all states. Nevertheless, it will often be the case that when the officer's privacy has been invaded, the family's privacy will have been invaded to the same or a similar extent. Thus, for example, where a listening device is unlawfully planted in the officer's home, the officer's spouse and children have suffered an invasion of their own privacy, even though the officer was the primary target of the electronic surveillance. Consequently, if the right of privacy is recognized at all in that jurisdiction, the family members should have spearate actions for the tort.[9]

f. Other Indirect Injuries to Family Members.

The types of action mentioned above are examples only. In general, it may be said that whenever a family member has suffered as a result of an action directed at the officer, the possibility arises that the family member may have a separate tort action in his or her own right. This possibility should be carefully explored by counsel, even though the damage to the family member appears slight and even though the action was directed at the officer rather than at the family member.

g. Direct Injuries to Family Members.

In addition, it goes without saying that *whenever a family member has been directly and deliberately harmed, the family member has a cause of action in tort, even though the ultimate purpose of the action was to put pressure on or cause distress to the officer.* Thus, for example, if someone beats an officer's wife or child for the purpose of causing distress to the officer, the wife or child — as well as the officer — will have a right to recover damages against the perpetrator of the act. Such incidents are, fortunately, rare, but when they occur the family member has the same rights of recovery as those enjoyed by any other citizen under standard tort law principles, and the officer may also have a separate action as a member of the injured person's family.[10]

It should be noted by family members considering action against the person who injured or killed the officer that, in the event of a recovery against the wrongdoer, any pension benefits paid to the family as a result of the injury or death may have to be repaid in whole or part. (See the discussion of the "collateral source" rule in Chapter 4.)

3. *Class Actions*

Under certain circumstances, an officer may be able to sue not only on his own behalf, but also on behalf of other officers. Where an entire identifiable group of officers — for example, all of the members of a department — have been injured or are about to be injured by the behavior of the defendant, one or a few members of the group may file what is known as a "class action" — an action for the benefit of themselves and the other members of the group or "class." [11]

Certain requirements may have to be met before an officer can bring a class action. The rules vary from jurisdiction to jurisdiction. The Federal Rules of Civil Procedure provide that:

> One or more members of a class may sue or be sued as representative parties on behalf of all only if (1) the class is so numerous that joinder of all members is impracticable, (2) there are questions of law or fact common to the class, (3) the claims or defenses of the representative parties are typical of the claims or defenses of the class, and (4) the representative parties will fairly and adequately protect the interests of the class.[12]

(The rule prescribes additional requirements as well.)

Despite such attempts to limit the number of class actions, this legal device has become very popular in some fields of the law, including civil rights. However, it does not as yet appear to have been used extensively by police officers in suits against persons outside of their departments. Probable

49

causes for this relative lack of use include the often-present procedural limitations of the type illustrated in the Federal Rule, and the fact that most attacks on the police are individual in nature, and do not involve officers as a class.

One obvious exception to this is the growing number of cases involving libel or slander of police; statements or articles derogating entire departments, or law enforcement personnel in general, are becoming common.[13] Unfortunately, there is a rule of law which renders the class action unavailable in such cases. This rule states that where a large group of persons is defamed, and no individual or individuals are specifically identified, no member or members of that group may bring a defamation suit either as an individual action or as a class action. Thus, for example, where two members of the Dallas County (Texas) sheriff's department brought a class action for defamation on behalf of the "deputies, agents, and employees" of the department, a group consisting of over seven hundred people, the court dismissed the action, stating that the plaintiffs

> ... may not recover damages for defamation of a group or class in excess of 740 persons ....[14]

Thus, in the very type of case in which the class action would be most useful to police officers, a technical rule of law prevents the use of that type of suit.[15]

4. *Actions by Police Associations*

In many instances, suits are being brought by police associations in the name of the association, on behalf of one or more officers. Many of these suits are, in effect, class actions, although they may not be labeled as such, since the associations are acting as the representative of their members.

Having the association act as plaintiff in the litigation may be advantageous for a number of reasons, including the efficiency of consolidation of actions and the fact that the burden of legal fees and costs is then borne by the association, rather than by the individual officers.[16]

The Los Angeles and New York area police associations, for example, have reportedly been bringing actions in this manner.[17]

Courts are not always willing to allow police associations to act as plaintiffs, either on behalf of or in addition to individual police officers. In some instances, the associations have been summarily dismissed as parties to the suits on the grounds that the associations lack standing to sue on behalf of individual plaintiffs.[18]

Police associations should note that whenever the association has itself paid financial benefits to the injured officer as a result of the injury, *the association may then be able to sue the person who caused the injury under the principle of subrogation.* In this event, the association will be suing not as a representative of the officer, or in the officer's behalf, but in the association's own right, to recover the association's own funds.[19]

5. *Actions by Governmental Bodies Employing Injured Officers*

Under certain circumstances, the city or state which employs the injured officer may be able to bring suit against the person who caused the injury. This possibility has often been ignored by the governmental bodies concerned. This is unfortunate, because the death or disabling injury of a police officer may cause serious financial loss to the city or state involved. This loss may include, for example, (1) medical bills, (2) sick pay, (3) funeral expenses, and (4) pensions and/or lump sum death benefits to the spouse and/or children of a deceased officer. In addition, the employing agency will be forced to recruit and train a replacement for the lost officer — which can, in itself, be an expensive process.

51

Since this loss is ultimately borne by the taxpayers, it would seem that the city or other employing body should be obligated to attempt to recoup these losses from the actual wrongdoer whenever possible.

There appear to be three major bases for a claim by the city against the wrongdoer, as follows:

    a. The common-law right of the employer to sue for injury to an employee;

    b. The right of subrogation for amounts paid to the employee in benefits as a result of the injury;

    c. The right to seek compensation for damage to city property or for other expenses not related to employee benefits but incurred by the city as a result of the defendant's behavior.

These will now be considered in turn.

a. Direct Action for Injury to the Employee.

The common law of England recognized a right of tort action by the master when a servant was injured by the wrongful act of another. This action was based upon the idea that the master had, by the wrongful act of the defendant, been deprived of the services of the servant. This was, consequently, a separate action, belonging solely to the master, and independent of any right of action which the injured servant might have against the defendant.

This independent action by the employer was widely allowed in the United States in the nineteenth century, but in recent decades many American courts have apparently declined to recognize it in the absence of a statute.

Nevertheless, a number of courts have specifically held that an employer may recover for loss of services when an employee has been injured,[20] and others have acknowledged the existence of the right indirectly in dictum.[21] At least two states, Oklahoma and California, have statutes expressly establishing this right of action.[22]

52

One difficulty which may be encountered in attempting to assert this right is the apparent confusion in the cases between the master's independent right of action for the loss of the servant's services and the separate right of action under subrogation principles when the employer has paid benefits to the injured employee. (Subrogation is defined and discussed further in the next section.) The confusion is understandable, since the damages for loss of services of course include benefits paid, but the actual cost to the employer of the loss of services is not necessarily limited to benefits paid; there are often other costs, such as the cost of obtaining and training a replacement, mentioned previously, which are not covered under subrogation.

This failure to distinguish between rights obtained by the employer through subrogation and the employer's independent cause of action for loss of services may be responsible for many of the decisions denying the employer an action for loss of services. (Indeed, in many of the cases now coming before the courts it is difficult to determine whether the city is proceeding under a theory of subrogation or upon the independent cause of action for loss of services.)

Confusion is not, of course, the only basis upon which American courts have denied the right of action; many have apparently simply felt that the concept is outmoded or unnecessary. Nevertheless, city attorneys contemplating an action for injuries to police officers should consider the possibility that unfavorable previous decisions have been based in part upon a failure to distinguish clearly the basis for the claim, and should draft their pleadings so that the action for loss of services is not confused with rights obtained by subrogation.[23]

b. Action by the Employer by Right of Subrogation.

Under certain circumstances, the municipality may be able to bring action against the wrongdoer under the concept known as "subrogation." "Subrogation" may be defined as follows: "The substitution of one person in the place of another with reference to a lawful claim, demand or right . . . so that he who is substituted succeeds to the rights of the other. . . ." [24]

Under this concept, when an officer has been injured, and the city has paid the officer's medical bills, etc., the city may then in effect step into the legal shoes of the injured officer and assert the right of recovery that the officer could have asserted against the wrongdoer, at least to the extent of the city's payments to the officer.

Procedurally, the city may recover its costs (a) by paying the benefits to the officer and suing the defendant independently for the amount expended; [25] (b) by intervening in a suit already brought by the officer; [26] or (c) by enforcing a repayment requirement against an officer who has already recovered from the defendant.[27]

Unfortunately for the municipalities involved, the right of subrogation is not recognized in all jurisdictions. Those that do allow this form of recovery by the employer base the right upon one of the following:

(1) *Statute.*

A number of states have statutes which specifically permit the city to recover costs in this manner.[28] (These same statutes may, however, place limitations on the city's subrogation rights.[29])

(2) *Contract.*

Even in the absence of statute, a city may obtain subrogation rights by virtue of a contractual agreement with the injured person. Thus, for example, if benefits are accepted by the injured officer under the express condition that the officer's rights are to that extent thereby subrogated to the city, the city could then proceed against the defendant wrongdoer to recover the amount paid, or could require the officer to reimburse the city to that extent.[30]

(3) *Equitable Subrogation.*

The common law, or, more accurately, the early courts of equity, recognized a right of subrogation whenever one was legally obligated to pay debts or expenses of another, or was forced to do so to protect his own interests, or was requested by the debtor to make the payment. The states have generally not recognized this equitable right of subrogation in the absence of statute or contract. An annotation in A.L.R.2d [31] declares that Pennsylvania is the only jurisdiction which has permitted subrogation under equitable principles in the absence of statute. Although Pennsylvania may not now be the only state which recognizes the principle of subrogation in the absence of statute or contract, there are in fact several cases in which Pennsylvania cities have been permitted to recover for benefits paid to police officers under an equitable subrogation theory.[32]

It should be remembered that, under any theory, there can be no subrogation unless the city was *obligated* to pay the benefits. Gratuitous payments not required to be made by the employer do not give rise to a right of subrogation. Furthermore, even if the city should be entitled to recover, any amounts expended by the officer in obtaining a judgment or settlement — *e.g.,* attorney's fees — would have to be deducted from the amount being returned to the city.[33]

For additional cases and information regarding subrogation, see the sources cited in the footnote.[34]

It should be noted that, although the employing municipality's rights are of benefit to the taxpayers who would otherwise foot the bill, these rights do, in the case of subrogation at least, result in a deduction from the officer's own recovery from the wrongdoer. While this is not entirely unreasonable — since otherwise the officer would, in effect, have a double recovery for the injury — it does mean that officers who bring suit in jurisdictions which permit subrogation may recover smaller total amounts than those who sue in jurisdictions which do not permit subrogation and thereby allow, in effect, a double recovery.

In this same connection, see also the discussion of the "collateral source" rule in Chapter 4.

c. Action by the Employer for Damages to the Employer's Property and Other Expenses.

The same incident which results in personal injury to the individual officer may also result in damage to the city's property or may cause the city to incur expenses other than the payment of benefits to an injured officer. For example, the automobile crash which injures the officer may result in damage to the patrol car in which the officer was riding; [35] or a false distress call may cause heavy expense to the city in terms of damage to or use or expenditure of resources or supplies.[36] The city or state may therefore have a cause of action in its own right for its losses or expenses, exclusive of and in addition to any action for benefits paid to an injured officer.

d. Contract Actions by the Employer.

Under some circumstances, the city may have an action *in contract* against someone whose breach of a contract with the city resulted in injury to police personnel. For example, a breach of a contract to keep vehicles in good repair, or to provide effective safety equipment, which led to injury could be actionable.[37]

6. *Actions by Insurance Companies for Injuries to Insured Officers*

The concept of subrogation may also give a right of action against the wrongdoer to an insurance company which has insured the life or health of an injured or killed officer. This may occur as the result of an individual policy obtained by the officer, or a group policy obtained by the employer.

These subrogation rights are, of course, contractual in nature. The states have generally recognized the validity of such contractual subrogation provisions, at least in the case of medical and disability insurance plans.[38] Subrogation rights have not generally been enforced in connection with life insurance policies, because of technical legal obstacles and a general agreement among companies writing life insurance not to pursue subrogation claims.

The problems of insurance subrogation are complex and are adequately treated in other volumes; it is sufficient here simply to point out that the insurer may have a right of subrogation against the defendant or against any recovery obtained independently by the officer, if the contract of insurance so provides.[39]

The foregoing list of potential plaintiffs is not intended to be exclusive; a particular factual situation may give rise to rights of action in persons or organizations other than those mentioned here. Furthermore, the lengthy discussion of rights of action by employing municipalities should not be allowed to obscure the fact that the primary emphasis of this book is upon compensation of the injured officer, not the injured city or taxpayer. To the injured officer, the primary question is usually the second one asked at the beginning of this chapter: "Who can be sued?" We will therefore now examine the problem of determining the number and identity of the potential defendants in the injured officer's proposed civil action.

B. DEFENDANTS—WHO CAN BE SUED?

It is both elementary and obvious that officers planning a civil suit must decide in advance who the defendants will be. In some cases, this is easily determined; in others, it can be a very difficult question. In either type of case it is critical, for, if the wrong person is named as the defendant, the case may be dismissed before the officer even has a chance to present the facts to a jury. Furthermore, as will shortly appear, in many instances there will be several — perhaps many — persons other than the actual assailant who are liable for the injury. Failure to include these additional defendants in the suit may cause the suit to fail or render a favorable verdict useless. The discussion which follows is therefore one of the most significant (perhaps the most significant) single section of this book.

1. *The Actual Assailant*

In most cases in which a police officer has been the victim of a tortious act, there will be one individual who is the visible and immediate perpetrator of the wrongful act, for example, the person who fires the shot at the officer or the person who utters the defamatory words against the officer.[40] Obviously these persons will, if the act was without legal justification, be held civilly responsible, and this will be true even if other persons are found also to be liable under the principles discussed in the next section. *The person who actually commits the wrongful act will therefore normally be a party defendant in the civil action without regard to the presence or absence of other defendants.*

If one had merely to file the action against the immediate actor, the selection of defendants would be simple and this chapter would end here. However, there are two problems which make further analysis necessary. First of all, in many instances there will be more than one person directly involved in the assault — as, for example, where the officer is attacked by a group of people, or where a number of persons utter the same defamatory statements. Which one

58

— or ones — are the "actual assailants"? This is particularly perplexing when the attack is made pursuant to a complex plan in which different persons participate to different degrees. Which of the participants will be held accountable by the law?

In addition, the actual individual assailant, although easily identifiable as such, may be (and often is) financially unable to satisfy even the most modest civil judgment, even if one is obtained — a condition referred to by lawyers as being "judgment proof." It therefore becomes critically important to determine if others besides the assailant are subject to civil liability for the act, for the additional defendants may have the financial assets to satisfy the judgment, whereas the actual assailant may not.

2. *Other Persons Legally Responsible for the Act of the Assailant*

a. Theories of Liability.

There are several bases upon which additional persons may be held liable for an act which they themselves did not personally commit.

(1) Liability may be based upon the additional defendant's *own wrongdoing,* as where the additional party encouraged the commission of an intentional tort, or was himself guilty of some prior negligence which, combined with the later and more visible negligence of another, led to the injury.

(2) The additional defendant's liability may be *vicarious,* by which is meant simply that although the person in question was not guilty of any personal wrongdoing, he or she will be held financially responsible by the law for policy reasons. Such liability is therefore only technical, and is not based upon any actual fault of

the person being held vicariously liable, but is imposed for some purpose deemed socially desirable by the courts. Thus, for example, vicarious liability may be imposed in a particular situation to encourage greater care by all persons involved in that activity; or, as is most often the case, vicarious liability will be imposed upon someone, such as an employer, who is more likely to be financially solvent than the actual wrongdoer, so that the injured plaintiff will be assured of a "deep pocket" from which compensation for the plaintiff's injuries can be obtained.

This concept of vicarious liability is of special importance to the police plaintiff, for it often provides a source from which a judgment can be satisfied when the actual wrongdoer is indigent and therefore judgment proof.

(3) A third possible basis for third-party liability is contractual. Some person or organization — such as an insurance company — may, by contract, have agreed to be responsible financially for the behavior of the attacker. In the past, this has seldom arisen in the police context, but it is perhaps potentially of more importance than has been generally realized up to this time. (Specific examples based upon each of these types of liability are discussed below.)

Whatever the basis of liability, the point to remember is that many persons besides the immediate actor may be made party defendants in civil actions, and since these additional defendants often possess financial resources which the actual assailant lacks, the ability to identify potential additional defendants may make the difference between success and failure of the action. If the named defendants have no assets, the officer (a) may never be able to persuade an attorney to bring the action at all, or (b) may be unable to collect a judgment if and when one is obtained.

Selection of defendants is critical to the officer's cause.

b. Categories of Defendants.

(1) *Groups.*

In tort law, all those who participate in, aid and abet, or even encourage the commission of the tort are normally liable for the results to the same extent as the person who strikes the blow, utters the false accusation, etc. Thus, where more than one person is actively involved in the perpetration of a tort, *all* are frequently liable.

Suppose, for example, that four persons, *A, B, C,* and *D,* decide to beat up an officer. Obviously, if *A, B, C,* and *D* all go to ambush the officer and all four strike him, they are all liable for the battery. An *equal degree* of participation is not necessary to hold all four liable, however. Thus, suppose that *A* helps plan the ambush but stays home on the night of the attack. *B, C,* and *D* accost the officer; *B* does not touch the officer but keeps a lookout for other police patrols and prevents spectators from interfering; *C* holds the officer; and *D* strikes the officer. *A, B, C,* and *D* are all jointly and severally liable for the injury.[41]

The same principles apply even where no prior agreement or conspiracy exists between the parties, as where a crowd gathers spontaneously and attacks an officer without prior planning.

Generally speaking, a mere spectator to an attack will not be held liable. Thus, in the previous example of the spontaneously-gathered crowd, if some members of the crowd attack the officer while others merely stand by and watch without actively encouraging or aiding the attackers in any way, the spectators normally will not be liable even though they may be privately sympathetic to the attackers.

If, however, the group is *engaged in an illegal activity* at the time of the attack, all members of the group may be held liable for the injury even though the members of the group

61

other than the actual attacker were mere spectators to the attack and did not participate in or encourage it in any way.[42]

Under certain circumstances, an organization may be held liable for tort injuries, as may the leaders and individual members of the organization. For example, an organization which advocates violence as a matter of policy may be held liable if members of that group engage in violence in response to that policy.[43]

The principle applies to nonviolent torts as well. For example, an organization whose leaders utter libelous or slanderous statements may be held responsible for the defamation,[44] and in at least one case an officer has reportedly brought suit against a civic club for defamatory remarks made about the officer during a club meeting.[45] Similar principles of group liability apply when the injury was due to negligence rather than being intentional. For example, if several drivers engage in a drag race, as a result of which an officer is injured or killed, all those participating will be liable even though only one car was involved in the collision which caused the actual injury.[46]

(2) *Employers of Wrongdoers.*

The employer of the actual tort-feasor may be held liable on several theories.

The most common basis for liability is the rule, well established in tort law, that the employer is vicariously liable for the wrongful act of an employee committed within the scope of the employment. This is, of course, technical liability imposed for policy reasons upon the employer, who is entirely innocent of any personal wrongdoing. This rule, known as the doctrine of *respondeat superior* (which, loosely translated, means "get the boss") may be invoked by the plaintiff to ensure that someone with sufficient financial assets to satisfy a judgment will be a defendant in the suit. It applies whether the tort was negligent or intentional, as

62

long as the act was performed "within the scope of the employment" as that term is used in tort and agency law.[47]

The employer may also be liable for injuries inflicted upon an officer by an employee where the employer or employing organization has itself been negligent in some manner connected with the employee's activities. For example, if an employer negligently hires an unfit person, or negligently fails to train the employee properly, or fails to supervise the employee adequately, the employer will be liable. This is not vicarious liability, but the employer's own negligence.[48] (Naturally, if one person hires another for the specific purpose of injuring or killing an officer, the employer will be liable as an intentional tort-feasor. Most of the cases, however, involve negligence.)

One major advantage to the officer-plaintiff in obtaining a judgment against the employer is the possibility that the employer, in addition to having substantial tangible assets, is often heavily insured against liability for the acts of employees. (See (5) *infra.*)

(3) *Persons Having Custody of, Control Over, or Responsibility for the Tort-Feasor.*

Persons who are charged by law with the custody or control of another person may be held responsible when the person subject to their control or custody commits a tort. For example, the parents of an underage person who causes injury may be liable for the act of the child.[49] This may be vicarious liability, based upon common-law doctrines or upon statutes, or it may be liability based upon the parents' own failure to supervise the child properly. (Parents may also be liable for injuries resulting when they have given the child a dangerous instrument, such as a gun or knife, or have permitted the child to retain such an instrument acquired from someone else. See Section (6) *infra.*)

63

Other custodians may be responsible for the behavior of
their charges. For example, the warden of a prison who
negligently allows a dangerous prisoner to go free, or the
superintendent of a mental hospital who negligently permits
the release or escape of a dangerous mental patient, may be
held responsible for acts committed by the prisoner or
patient while free.[50] This rule applies, however, only when
it is "foreseeable" that the plaintiff will be injured; thus, for
example, if the custodian was not aware of the violent
tendencies of the person released, there may be no liability.[51]

(4) *Premises Owners, Lessees, Etc.*

When an officer is injured, whoever owns, leases, occupies,
or conducts commercial enterprises or other activities upon
the premises where the injury occurred may be legally
responsible for the injury.

Obviously, if the owner, lessee, etc. (hereafter referred to
simply as the "owner" for the sake of brevity) personally
assaults the officer or orders the officer assaulted, there will
be liability. Furthermore, we have already discussed the
doctrine of *respondeat superior,* under which an employer is
liable for the tort of the employee committed within the scope
of the employment.

In addition, however, a premises owner may be held liable
to an injured officer in at least two instances:

(a) Where there is a physical defect in the premises
(for example, a rotten floorboard) which causes the
injury to the officer; and

(b) Where the officer is injured upon the premises by
a third party, whose wrongful and injurious act the
premises owner should have prevented. (This liability of
the premises owner may arise whether the act of the
third party was negligent or intentional.) Both types of
injuries are discussed in detail in Chapter 5.[52]

64

As with employers, insurance carried by premises owners may provide a readily available source of judgment satisfaction.

(5) *Insurance Companies.*

In most jurisdictions, insurance companies are not normally named as defendants to the action. The most common procedure is to name the insured person or organization as the defendant, whereupon the insurer, if any, will be contractually obligated to defend the case on behalf of the insured and pay any judgment which is obtained. However, in some jurisdictions, under certain types of policies, or in certain circumstances, it may be possible — or necessary — for the plaintiff to sue the insurance company directly as a named defendant, and so insurance companies may properly be included in this listing.[53]

Whether the insurance company is sued directly or is merely obligated to pay a judgment against the actual wrongdoer, the existence of insurance covering the defendant is a matter of extreme importance to the plaintiff officer. This is a consideration which is all too often overlooked. Plaintiff's counsel in an auto crash will, of course, expect the presence of liability insurance, but insurance coverage may be available in many other situations, and it seems probable that this has not always been fully appreciated and explored by counsel contemplating a prospective client's chances of ultimate recovery.

For example, homeowners, businesses (including both retail merchants, manufacturers, and other types of enterprise), and professional people often carry insurance which may cover the particular injury suffered by the officer. In most instances, this insurance will be applicable only to negligent injuries, and will not cover intentional wrongs, but, as will be noted in the chapter dealing with

65

tactical considerations (Chapter 11), many injuries involve aspects of both negligence and intent, and the resulting lawsuit may often be brought on either or both theories. The possibility that some insurance policy may include coverage of the defendant's wrongful act should always be explored thoroughly by counsel, by independent investigation or, if necessary, in discovery procedures.

In addition, of course, the officer may himself be carrying insurance which protects the officer in the event of injury by others. Uninsured motorists insurance and medical payments insurance under the officer's own automobile policy may be applicable; hospitalization, disability, and accident policies or (as noted earlier) workmen's compensation plans may also apply. Usually, of course, the officer will not be reduced to suing the officer's *own* insurance carrier, but such suits are occasionally necessary when there is a dispute as to coverage.[54]

(6) *Vendors, Donors, and Custodians of Dangerous Instruments and Liquor.*

It has already been noted that parents who provide their offspring with dangerous implements, such as guns or knives, may be liable when the recipient of the dangerous instrument employs it unlawfully to injure another. The same principle applies to vendors or donors other than parents. Since this point of law is often covered by statute, it is difficult to generalize; however, the plaintiff officer should be aware that, depending upon local law, one or more of the following rules may be applicable.

(a) Those who sell weapons or explosives to unfit persons (*e.g.,* to one who is obviously intoxicated) may be held liable for misuse of the item.[55] This is especially true where the sale is in violation of a statute (for example, a statute prohibiting sale of firearms to minors). The same rule may apply to gifts, although the

66

statutes more often specifically apply to commercial sales.

(b) So-called "dram shop acts" may make the owner or employees of a bar or other establishment which dispenses alcoholic beverages liable for injury done by the persons to whom the alcohol is sold, particularly where the purchaser was obviously already intoxicated at the time of the sale. Even private persons providing drinks in a noncommercial setting (for example, the host at a party) may be liable in some jurisdictions.

(c) Those owning or having custody of dangerous instruments who negligently allow the instruments to fall into the wrong hands may be liable for subsequent misuse of the instruments. Thus, for example, it has been held that a parking lot owner could be sued by an officer injured when an automobile was stolen from the lot and subsequently struck the officer.[56] By analogy, any person charged with the safekeeping of any dangerous implement, who negligently permits that implement to be stolen or otherwise improperly removed from its designated location, might be held liable if the instrument is thereafter used to injure the plaintiff. For example, one who, being under a duty to keep a weapon safely under lock and key, negligently allows a dangerous person to remove the weapon from its place of custody, might be held liable to an officer subsequently shot with that weapon.[57]

(7) *Governmental Bodies and Employees.*

In some instances an officer may wish to bring suit against a governmental body, such as a city, in connection with an injury.[58] Litigation against governmental bodies and employees can be very complex, but the following brief summary may be helpful.

67

(a) Sovereign Immunity. Governmental bodies may be protected from suit by the doctrine of "sovereign immunity." At common law, the sovereign could not be held civilly responsible for its activities and could therefore not be named as a defendant in a tort action. However, the federal government, and many state governments, have waived all or part of that immunity by legislative act, so that they can now be named as defendants in many types of tort actions.

Municipal corporations were, even at common law, immune only as to certain "governmental" activities and even this limited immunity is being eliminated in many jurisdictions today. Furthermore, even where the doctrine of sovereign immunity is still recognized, that immunity may be lost if the government has engaged in a criminal act.[59]

Any officer wishing to hold a governmental body liable for a tort will first have to determine whether the doctrine of sovereign immunity still applies in that particular situation and jurisdiction.

(b) Theories of Liability. Assuming that the governmental body in question does not enjoy sovereign immunity in the action, it can then be sued as any other defendant. This liability may be based upon several theories, including the following:

(i) *Liability for the Act of an Official or Employee of the City Which Causes Direct Injury to the Officer.* Examples might include a city employee assaulting the officer, or negligently striking the officer with a city vehicle; or a city official uttering defamatory statements about the officer.[60] (Governmental officials may be protected by a personal privilege in defamation cases; this privilege is independent of the "sovereign immunity" doctrine discussed above. See Chapter 8.)

Injuries inflicted by another police officer may or may not be actionable. Where the plaintiff officer has been injured by an officer from another jurisdiction, no problem will normally be encountered; [61] but where the injury has been caused by an officer of the plaintiff's own department, problems may arise in suing the department because of the so-called "fellow servant rule" and the restrictions of the applicable workmen's compensation law, at least where the officer who caused the injury was acting within the scope of the employment. (Where the injury was not within the scope of the employment, the city will of course normally not be liable anyway, and the plaintiff officer may have to bring the action solely against the other officer.) [62]

(ii) *Liability for the Act or Omission of City Employees Which Results in Injury to the Officer by a Third Party.* In some instances, officers who have been injured by the criminal or negligent act of third persons have attempted to add the city, state, or other governmental body which employs the officer as a party defendant, based upon the theory that the negligence act or omission of the governmental body has been a contributing cause of the injury. These negligent acts or omissions might take several forms, including:

(a) Failure to supervise premises or persons under the city or state's control; [63]

(b) Failure to train, equip, or support the injured officers properly or to establish proper procedures to ensure their safety while on duty.[64]

These arguments have not always been met with sympathy by the courts in specific cases.[65] Nevertheless, it would seem that, under general tort principles, *any* defendant, governmental or otherwise, who negligently creates a condition in which it is *foreseeable* that the criminal intervention of a third party will result may be held liable for that negligence.[66]

(8) *Other Defendants; Organized Crime Syndicates.*

In addition to the types of defendants listed above, there

69

will be many other situations in which one person is liable for the act of another, either vicariously or through some related personal fault. For example, the publisher of a libel or slander may be responsible for repetitions of the defamation by others (see Chapter 8), and, as already noted, *anyone* whose negligent conduct creates a foreseeable risk that a third party will cause injury to the plaintiff may be held liable along with the immediate assailant.

One interesting possibility has been the suggestion, made in a recent magazine article, that organized crime syndicates may be held civilly liable for actions of their minions.[67]

3. *Attorneys*

Most officers will be interested to learn that in certain specific situations, it may be possible to bring suit against attorneys. Of course, whenever an attorney commits any of the torts discussed in Chapters 5-9, the attorney may usually be sued as any other defendant.[68] However, two situations are of special note:

a. The officer's own attorney is, of course, liable for any negligence in the handling of the officer's case. Failure to file suit on behalf of the officer within the period allowed by the statute of limitations, for example, will usually render the attorney liable to the officer for the damages that would have been recoverable from the assailant.

b. Where the officer has been the victim of an unjustified civil or criminal action, the attorney who brought the suit against the officer may be liable for malicious prosecution, false arrest, defamation, or some related tort.

Medical doctors have been responsible for some significant developments in this field. Physicians are now bringing suits against the attorneys of patients who have filed medical malpractice actions against them. These suits are usually for malicious prosecution, but other tort theories, such as defamation, infliction of mental distress, abuse of process, and negligence are being attempted, and recoveries are being obtained.[69]

In view of the extraordinary number of baseless civil actions currently being filed against police officers, it would appear that at least some of the attorneys involved might be held liable to the officer upon the same principles.

(For additional discussion of malicious prosecution suits against attorneys, see Chapter 7.)

4. *Suits Against the Officer's Own Department or Supervisors*

As previously noted, this book does not include within its scope disputes between the officer and the officer's own supervisors arising out of questions of employment, promotion, discipline, discrimination, etc., which are the basis for most litigation between such parties.

As discussed earlier, however, if some member of the officer's own department commits a *tort* against the officer, the department, supervisor, or fellow officer may certainly be named as a defendant, subject to applicable statutes, regulations, and rules of law. The bulk of the known *tort* actions against the officer's own department or supervisors have involved defamatory remarks by a department official, although direct personal injuries or negligence leading to foreseeable injuries by third persons have sometimes been the basis for such actions.[70]

The moral, then, of this chapter is simply this: In every civil action, the plaintiff officer (and the officer's counsel) should examine the facts and the applicable law carefully to ensure that (1) all those who have been injured will be able to obtain compensation and (2) all those who are legally (and financially) responsible for the injury are joined in the action as defendants. As previously noted, failure to join all possible parties may mean a failure to obtain compensation; and a failure to obtain justified compensation is a failure of justice.

CHAPTER 3 — NOTES

1. *See,* for example, FED. R. CIV. P. 42.

2. *See* Section 2a below.

3. This procedure will normally be invoked by the relatives or friends of the officer, who must petition the court for appointment of a guardian to bring the action. It does not occur automatically.

4. *See* Section 5b below.

5. These separate rights of family members may be dependent upon the right of the injured officer to recover, however. *See,* for example, the discussion of wrongful death in Ch. 5 *infra,* and the discussion of other family rights, below.

6. Anson v. Fletcher, 192 Neb. 317, 220 N.W.2d 371, 378 (1974). Not all jurisdictions fully recognize this right. For example, in some states the statutes granting women equal rights have been construed to deprive the husband of any right of action when the wife is injured. On the other hand, the development of equal rights for women has led an increasing number of states to recognize the wife's separate right to sue for the injury to her husband, although some of these jurisdictions apparently allow this only where the injury was intentional. *See generally* PROSSER, LAW OF TORTS §§ 124-125 (4th ed. 1971).

7. As noted above, however, parents are usually included in the classes of survivors who may recover in wrongful death actions.

8. *See* Ch. 6 *infra.*

9. *See* Ch. 9 *infra.*

10. *See* Ch. 6 *infra,* and the discussion of intentional infliction of mental distress.

11. *See* BLACK'S LAW DICTIONARY (4th ed. 1951) for further definition.

12. FED. R. CIV. P. 23(a).

13. *See,* for example, the September 1977 issue of *Texas Monthly* magazine, in which an article entitled *Support Your Local Police (Or Else)* appeared. The cover of the magazine was a photograph depicting Houston police officers as motorcycle hoodlums, and bore the legends "New Gang in Town," and "What Happens When Cops Run Wild?"

14. Webb v. Sessions, 531 S.W.2d 211, 213 (Tex. Civ. App. 1975).

15. The rule is not, however, specifically designed to prevent class actions by police officers. The rule that members of a large group may not sue unless identified as individuals is long established in tort law, and is applied to all groups of whatever occupation.

16. *See* Ch. 2 *supra.*

17. *See, e.g.,* THE POLICE PLAINTIFF, 78-1, at 3, and 76-1, at 7.

18. *See, e.g.,* Los Angeles Fire & Police Protective League v. Rodgers, 7 Cal. App. 3d 419, 86 Cal. Rptr. 623 (1970). *See also* THE POLICE PLAINTIFF, 76-3, at 8.

19. Subrogation is discussed more fully in connection with employers, below.

20. *E.g.,* New York (Mineral Indus., Inc. v. George, 44 Misc. 2d 764, 255 N.Y.S.2d 114 (1965)).

21. *E.g.,* Texas (Houston Belt & Terminal Ry. v. Burmester, 309 S.W.2d 271 (Tex. Civ. App. 1957)).

22. 76 OKLA. STAT. ANN. § 8(4); CAL. CIV. CODE § 49(c).

23. For collected cases, *see* 57 A.L.R.2d 802 (1958). *See also* specific cases cited in the discussion of subrogation, below.

24. BLACK'S LAW DICTIONARY 1595 (4th ed. 1951).

25. *See, e.g.,* THE POLICE PLAINTIFF, 76-1, at 12, reporting two Los Angeles Superior Court cases, City of Los Angeles v. Gant, Civ. No. 17441, in which the city recovered $121,289.12; and City of Los Angeles v. Miller, Civ. No. 931767, in which the city was awarded $65,472.06.

26. *See, e.g.,* Hinman v. Westinghouse Elec. Co., 88 Cal. Rptr. 188, 471 P.2d 988 (1970).

27. *See, e.g.,* Beca v. Mayor & City Council, 279 Md. 177, 367 A.2d 478 (1977).

28. *See* Smith v. County of Los Angeles, 276 Cal. App. 2d 156, 81 Cal. Rptr. 120 (1969) (officer killed in traffic accident, city entitled under CAL. LAB. CODE § 3201 *et seq.* to recover from tort-feasor's employer the pension benefits paid to officer's heirs). *See also, e.g.,* VA. CODE § 32-140.

29. *See* Richmond v. Hanes, 203 Va. 102, 122 S.E.2d 895 (1961), in which the court held that, despite a municipal personnel rule to the contrary, the city could not recover from the injured policeman's settlement fund any amount in excess of the statutory $700 limit.

30. *See* Beca v. Mayor & City Council, note 27 *supra.*

31. 70 A.L.R.2d 475, at 476-77 (1960).

32. *See, e.g.,* Topelski v. Universal S. Side Autos, Inc., 407 Pa. 339, 180 A.2d 414 (1962).

33. Furia v. City of Philadelphia, 180 Pa. Super. 50, 118 A.2d 236 (1955).

34. 70 A.L.R.2d 475 (1960); THE POLICE PLAINTIFF, 76-1, at 9-14; 77-3, at 9; 78-1, at 10-11. *See also* 42 U.S.C. §§ 2651-2653 (Medical Care Recovery Act).

35. *See, e.g.,* Sullivan v. Sudiak, 30 Ill. App. 3d 899, 333 N.E.2d 60 (1975); City of St. Petersburg v. Shannon, 156 So.2d 870 (Fla. App. 1963) (patrol cars wrecked in collisions).

36. *See* THE POLICE PLAINTIFF, 76-3, at 9-10.

37. *See* 86 A.L.R.2d 316 (1962) for a general discussion of contract actions of this type.

38. *See, e.g.,* Collins v. Blue Cross & Blue Shield, 213 Va. 540, 193 S.E.2d 782 (1973).

39. *See generally* 44 AM. JUR. 2d *Insurance* § 1820 *et seq.* (1969); 106 A.L.R. 1040 (1937).

40. Note that the terms "attacker," "assailant," etc., although most properly used in connection with intentional physical assaults on the officer, are here employed in connection with torts of all types — physical, verbal, etc. Thus, for the sake of convenience, one who, *e.g.,* utters slanderous statements about the officer, will be here included within the broader meaning of the terms "attacker" or "assailant."

41. For a further concise discussion of the general principles involved *see* PROSSER, LAW OF TORTS § 46 (4th ed. 1971).

42. A case of great significance on this point is Huckeby v. Spangler, 521 S.W.2d 568 (Tenn. 1975) (all persons "present at gambling establishments and participating knowingly and wilfully in violation of state gambling law when there was a discharge of firearms" which injured police officers could be held liable to injured officers for actions of those who fired the shots).

43. *See, e.g.,* THE POLICE PLAINTIFF, 78-1, at 3, reporting a suit filed by the Los Angeles police association against a political party which reportedly openly advocates violence, following injuries to several officers during a disturbance allegedly incited by members of the defendant organization. (Brazas v. Wagner, No. C204573, Superior Court, Los Angeles, Cal.) *See also* THE POLICE PLAINTIFF, 76-3, at 9, reporting the case of *Cardillo v. Dupree,* in which the family of a slain New York City police officer sued the Nation of Islam for acts allegedly committed by a member or members of the organization. (Police, including the plaintiff's deceased, were summoned to a building under the control of the defendant organization by an apparently fake distress call; Officer Cardillo was killed in the ensuing ambush.)

44. In NAACP v. Moody, 350 So.2d 1365 (Miss. 1977), the plaintiff officer recovered a trial court judgment of $210,000 against the NAACP for derogatory statements made about the officer by a spokesman for the group. (The case was reversed on appeal due to improper jury instructions.)

45. THE POLICE PLAINTIFF, 77-1, at 7, reporting the case of Rowley v. Placer Kiwanis Club, Superior Ct., Loomis County, Cal. (1976).

46. As to negligent joint tort-feasors generally, *see* PROSSER, LAW OF TORTS (4th ed. 1971).

47. In Hinman v. Westinghouse, 2 Cal. 3d 956, 471 P.2d 988 (1970), an officer recovered a judgment of $120,000 against an employer for an employee's negligent act.

48. Ironically, there has been a recent surge of litigation *against* police departments and police supervisors based upon these very same three principles: negligent hiring, negligent training, and negligent supervision. It seems fitting, therefore, that police officers invoke these rules in their own cases.

49. *See* Tabb v. Norred, 277 So.2d 223 (La. App. 1973) (minor shot officer, judgment rendered against minor's father and other defendants for $300,000); and Brechtel v. Lopez, 140 So.2d 189 (La. App. 1962) (officer injured in motor vehicle accident while pursuing son of defendant; officer awarded $22,500). *See also* THE POLICE PLAINTIFF, 76-1, at 12 and 77-3, at 4.

50. This general principle is well recognized, but many courts, while acknowledging the existence and validity of the general rule, have denied recovery under the facts of the individual case, usually on the grounds that the negligence of the warden was not the proximate cause of the ultimate injury. *See* 44 A.L.R.3d 899 (1972) and cases cited therein. In a recent case involving a police plaintiff, Frank v. Pitre, 353 So.2d 1293 (La. 1977), a sheriff released a prisoner from jail on pass. The prisoner, while free, shot the plaintiff officer who was trying to arrest him for creating a disturbance in a bar. The injured officer sued the sheriff on the grounds that the sheriff was negligent in releasing the prisoner. The plaintiff officer recovered a judgment of $40,000 which was affirmed by the Louisiana Court of Appeals. The Supreme Court of Louisiana reversed on the grounds that the sheriff's action "did not sufficiently contribute to the injury to create liability . . . ." (353 So.2d, at 1296.) The dissenting opinion in the case provides argument and authority in support of liability.

51. *See generally* 44 A.L.R.3d 899 (1972); *see also* THE POLICE PLAINTIFF, 77-3, at 4.

52. *See* Ch. 5, Section B *infra.*

53. The assailant's father's insurance company was a named defendant in Tabb v. Norred, note 49 *supra.*

54. *E.g.,* Dowden v. Liberty Mut. Ins. Co., 346 So.2d 1311 (La. App. 1977).

55. *The Police Plaintiff* reported that the pawn shop owner who sold a weapon to a customer who subsequently used it to shoot a police officer was named as a defendant in Forsdal v. McDonald, Superior Ct., Marin County, Cal. (1977). (THE POLICE PLAINTIFF, 77-3, at 4.)

56. Enders v. Apcoa, Inc., 55 Cal. App. 3d 897, 127 Cal. Rptr. 751 (1976).

57. Whether courts would recognize this liability in all such cases is doubtful. The *Enders* case (note 56 *supra*) indicated that liability would be imposed only where "special circumstances" made it foreseeable that the theft and subsequent injury to the plaintiff would occur. In addition, the court confined its discussion to stolen automobile cases. Nevertheless, it would seem that the principle should be applied in *any* case, regardless of the instrument involved, in which it was foreseeable that the instrument — weapon, automobile, explosives, etc. — might be stolen and used in a manner which would cause injury to the plaintiff. The principle is well established in tort law that the intervening criminal act of another will not relieve the defendant of liability *if the criminal intervention was "foreseeable."* For a general discussion, *see* PROSSER, LAW OF TORTS § 44 (4th ed. 1971).

58. This book does not deal with employment matters or other disputes of a contractual nature between officer and municipality. This discussion is concerned solely with possible tort liability of the city to the officer.

59. *See* Dill v. Rader, 533 P.2d 650 (Okla. App. 1975) (conspiracy by city officials to injure plaintiff officer).

60. Numerous cases of the latter type have been filed in recent years. They are discussed in connection with Defamation, Ch. 8 *infra*.

61. *See, e.g.,* THE POLICE PLAINTIFF, 78-1, at 3, reporting the case of Sarnie v. Prince Georges County (Cir. Ct. D.C. 1977) (plaintiff, a police officer of the District of Columbia, alleged that he had been beaten while being arrested in Maryland by a Maryland county officer).

62. *Cf.* Toler v. City of San Francisco, reported in THE POLICE PLAINTIFF, 78-1, at 3, in which the plaintiff officer, allegedly struck by a fellow officer during horseplay, filed suit against the city for $2,000,000. Presumably, a major issue in any such case would be whether the injury did in fact occur "within the scope of the employment."

63. As in Ward v. New York, 81 Misc. 2d 583, 366 N.Y.S.2d 800 (Ct. Cl. 1975), where two officers were wounded by an armed man on the grounds of a state hospital.

64. As in Cardillo v. Dupree, note 43 *supra*, in which the family of the slain officer reportedly named the police department and the city as defendants for "negligence in establishing and retaining a dangerous response procedure to 'officer in distress' calls."

65. In Ward v. New York, note 63 *supra*, the court dismissed the case against the state on the grounds that the state's negligence was not the "proximate cause" of the injury to the officers.

66. *See* discussion above, particularly note 57 *supra*.

67. Wennerholm, *Organized Criminals: Sue Them for Money,* THE POLICE CHIEF, Sept. 1977.

68. *See,* however, Ch. 8 *infra* regarding the attorney's privilege in defamation actions.

69. For an exhaustive discussion of the liability of attorneys to physicians for unfounded malpractice actions, *see* Birnbaum, *Physicians Counterattack: Liability of Lawyers for Instituting Unjustified Medical Malpractice Actions,* 45 FORDHAM L. REV. 1003 (1977). *See also* THE POLICE PLAINTIFF, 77-1, at 10, and 77-3, at 8.

70. Governmental employees also have a right to bring action against their employing agencies under the Civil Rights Act of 1970, 42 U.S.C. § 1983.

Chapter 4

FORMS OF RELIEF AVAILABLE

When the injured officer obtains legal counsel, the attorney will be responsible for determining what damages may be available to the officer, and will explain to the officer the type and amount of damages to be sought. Consequently, this chapter is intended only as a brief introduction to the general subject of civil damages; specific guidance will be provided by the plaintiff's attorney in each case.

In most instances in which a police plaintiff is bringing an action in tort, the object of the suit will be to obtain money damages. The bulk of the chapter is therefore devoted to a discussion of the type and amount of money damages which may be available.

In some instances, money damages may not be sufficient; the officer may find that something more is needed. Most superior trial courts are empowered to issue injunctions — *i.e.,* to order the defendant to do or not do some specific act — and this remedy will therefore also be discussed.

A. MONEY DAMAGES

1. *Types*

a. Compensatory Damages.

The primary object of tort law is to repay, or compensate, the injured plaintiff for the losses suffered because of the defendant's wrongdoing. The law of torts therefore provides that the injured plaintiff is entitled to receive whatever sum is necessary to "make good or replace the loss caused by the wrong or injury." [1] Compensatory damages are often referred to as "actual damages," because the purpose of compensatory damages is to repay the plaintiff for the injury actually suffered, and to put the plaintiff in as good a position as plaintiff occupied prior to the injury, at least to the extent that an award of money can accomplish that goal.

The items which may be considered in an award of compensatory damages vary greatly according to the type of tort action involved.

In personal injury actions, the elements of compensatory damage may include such items as:

(1) Actual expenses paid by the plaintiff or which the plaintiff may be obligated to pay. (These might include doctor and hospital bills, the cost of medicines, etc.)

(2) Lost income, both past and future.

(3) Pain and suffering, both past and future.

(4) Mental anguish, at least where accompanied by physical pain and suffering.[2]

In wrongful death cases, damages may be limited by the applicable statute, but will usually include amounts for medical bills and funeral expenses; the value of the financial support which the survivors would have received from the deceased had he or she not been killed; and compensation for the loss of the society, etc. of the deceased person.

In a property damage case, the plaintiff will normally be permitted to recover the difference between the fair market value of the property before and after the injury.

In defamation actions, the recovery is based upon the extent to which the plaintiff's reputation has suffered in the community, and may include not only actual pecuniary loss but mental suffering as well.[3]

If the defendant has aggravated an existing injury, as where a doctor negligently treats the plaintiff's injury, the doctor — and probably the person who caused the original injury — will be liable for the aggravation.

Attorney's fees are *not* normally recoverable as compensatory damages, but may be available in certain instances already discussed.[4]

The *amounts* awardable as compensatory damages vary widely, according to the nature and extent of the injury. In some instances, such as wrongful death, statutes may prescribe a set limit, but in most cases the extent of compensatory damages is limited only by what the plaintiff can show to the jury. Medical expenses can run into many thousands of dollars; loss of future income alone may, in the case of total disablement of a young person, easily exceed a million dollars; and the element of pain and suffering is so vague that an award for that item is limited only by the extent of the jury's sympathy for the plaintiff. Multimillion dollar judgments are becoming commonplace.[5]

b. Punitive Damages.

Punitive damages, often called exemplary damages, are damages awarded over and above the amount necessary to compensate the plaintiff for actual damage suffered. Punitive damages may be awarded to the plaintiff "... where the wrong done to him was aggravated by circumstances of violence, oppression, malice, fraud, or wanton and wicked conduct on the part of the defendant ...."[6]

Punitive damages are usually recoverable in intentional tort actions, such as battery and malicious prosecution; they are available in defamation actions where actual malice can be shown; and may even be awarded in negligence actions if the act of the defendant was not merely simple negligence but included wanton or reckless behavior. (Punitive damages are not, however, normally available in wrongful death actions, where only the elements of damage specified in the statute may be awarded.)

There are several different justifications which are offered for the allowance of punitive damages in a tort action. It is said that, although the tort law system is designed primarily for compensation and not punishment, the system allows punitive damages in certain cases (1) to punish a defendant whose behavior has been particularly vicious, aggravated, or flagrant and (2) to serve as an example to dissuade others from engaging in such reprehensible behavior. In addition, some jurisdictions have justified the award of punitive damages on the grounds that the plaintiff thereby obtains additional compensation not awardable under the recognized categories of compensatory damages in that jurisdiction. Finally, although it is not usually formally or publicly admitted, it is generally recognized that receipt of punitive damages enables the plaintiff to pay his attorney's fees — which may amount to one third or more of the total recovery — and still have enough left to cover the plaintiff's actual damages.

Many courts have stated that punitive damages are awardable only when actual damages have been awarded. This rule, which has in some instances been codified by state legislatures, is apparently based on a misunderstanding of earlier court opinions or statements in legal treatises. Clearly, in a negligence action, punitive damages cannot be awarded without an award of compensatory damages because *actual damage is an element of liability in negligence actions. There is no right of action at all in negligence unless there has been actual damage.* This is also true in some instances involving intentional torts, *e.g.,* trespass to chattels, which requires a showing of actual damage before there can be any liability at all. However, in most of the intentional tort actions, liability can be found *independent of the existence of actual damage.* Thus, a plaintiff may be entitled to a favorable verdict and an award of nominal damages (see below) in an action for battery, false imprisonment, trespass to land, etc., *even though no actual damage has been suffered by the plaintiff.* Thus, absent statute, there is no rule of law which precludes an award of punitive damages in those cases, despite the absence of actual damage.

Unfortunately, some courts (and legislatures) have misunderstood this, and have refused to give punitive damages even in cases of the latter type if no actual damages are found. Therefore, counsel practicing in such jurisdictions should attempt to find a basis for asserting some actual damage, however slight, in any action in which punitive damages are to be sought.[7]

The amount of punitive damages which can be awarded is virtually without limit, and depends upon the jury's view of the defendant's behavior and resources. If there is any limiting factor, it is the generally recognized principle that the award of punitive damages must bear some reasonable relation to the actual damage suffered, if any. In practice, punitive damage awards frequently amount to several times the amount of compensatory damages, and, in cases where punitive damages may be awarded without actual damage being suffered, the only limiting factor seems to be (a) the extent of the jury's disgust at the defendant's behavior and (b) the discretion of the court — which exists in all questions of damages — to set aside an award which the judge considers excessive.

Since one of the purposes of punitive damages is to punish, the financial resources of the defendant may properly be considered in determining what amount will be sufficient to accomplish the punitive goal. Therefore, an award of punitive damages which might be excessive if rendered against an individual may be perfectly proper if returned against a large corporation.[8]

c. Nominal Damages.

In some cases the plaintiff officer will have suffered no actual damage but will wish to bring the action as a matter of principle, or to vindicate the officer's own behavior. In certain tort actions, the defendant may be found at fault and a verdict returned to that effect even though there has been

83

no actual injury and therefore no compensatory damages can be awarded. These actions include assault, battery, conversion, false imprisonment, trespass to land, and other intentional torts discussed elsewhere in this book. In such actions, where liability is found but no compensatory damages can be awarded, the plaintiff is entitled to an award of "nominal" damages. This usually means that plaintiff will receive just a token amount, such as $1.00, as a gesture to indicate that the defendant has indeed been found at fault and the plaintiff's position has been vindicated. (Some courts have, however, viewed nominal damages simply as a small award for actual damage. See below.)

Punitive damages may also be available if nominal damages have been awarded, but, as noted in the preceding section, some courts have followed a contrary rule and allowed punitive damages only where actual damages have been awarded. Some courts confronted by this problem have avoided the difficulty by regarding "nominal" damages as being in fact a miniscule award of compensatory or "actual" damages, thus supporting the punitive damage award.[9]

2. Damage Awards in Police-Plaintiff Cases

a. Probability of Recovery.

Police officers contemplating civil suits often express doubt as to whether they will receive impartial consideration by judges and juries. Many officers feel that their status as policemen will cause them to be treated with hostility in the civil courtroom.

While comprehensive statistics are lacking, it appears that *if the case gets to the jury,* the police officer has, on the whole, approximately the same chance of receiving a favorable verdict as any other plaintiff. A 1974 study of 218 jury verdicts in personal injury cases involving police plaintiffs revealed that the plaintiff officers received a favorable verdict in 63 percent of the cases. The study noted that this was slightly below the national overall recovery rate for plaintiffs of all types, which is estimated at 65 percent.[10] However, in view of the limited size of the sample and the small degree of difference in the percentages, this is probably not a significant discrepancy. On the contrary, it seems that on the question of liability, the fact that the plaintiff is a police officer does not, overall, materially sway juries in either direction.

b. Size of Award.

The same study referred to in the preceding section found that, although the police plaintiff does not appear to recover any more or less often than nonpolice plaintiffs, when the police officer does recover a favorable verdict it is, on the average, likely to be substantially larger than awards made to other plaintiffs in similar cases. In fact, the researchers found that the awards juries gave to police plaintiffs "averaged 17% higher than the National Verdict Expectancies for similar injuries...." [11]

A study of cases in the author's own files in which police plaintiffs received money awards revealed the following:

(1) In cases which were settled prior to trial, the average settlement for all types of cases was $5,536.82 per case and $4,685.00 per officer. (Some of the cases involved more than one officer-plaintiff.)

(2) In cases which went to trial, the average recovery for all types of cases was $51,319.00 per case and $34,896.92 per officer. (Again, many cases involved multiple plaintiffs.)

(3) The average award in negligence cases for personal injuries was $39,097.20 per officer; the average award in intentional tort actions of which the majority were for battery, was $55,173.93 per officer; and the average award in defamation and false complaint cases was $18,143.48 per officer.

85

These figures should not be given too much weight by the reader because (1) the figures do not constitute a statistically reliable sample and (2) each case is highly individual in nature, so that averages are relatively meaningless to any one individual officer contemplating a civil action.[12] Nevertheless, the study indicates that officers can and do obtain substantial judgments in civil actions in amounts which often far exceed the limited benefits available under employers' compensation plans and in cases in which no such benefits are even available.

3. *Effect of Receipt of Benefits from Employer on Damages Recoverable from Defendant (the Collateral Source Rule)*

Since police officers are governmental employees and therefore normally receive some form of medical or disability benefits when injured, the question arises as to what effect the acceptance of these payments from the employer or the employer's insurance carrier will have upon the plaintiff's right to recover damages from the defendant.

The rule in most jurisdictions is that benefits received from any source independent of the defendant, even if these benefits in fact completely cover the plaintiff's actual damages, have no bearing upon the plaintiff's right to recover from the defendant, and *will not reduce the amount recoverable from the defendant.* Thus, the plaintiff officer who incurs $10,000 in medical bills and receives $10,000 in insurance benefits to cover those bills, may nevertheless recover an additional $10,000 from the defendant for those same medical expenses.

This principle of law is called the "collateral source" rule. It is often criticized as permitting a double recovery by the plaintiff for the same injury, but a majority of American jurisdictions have taken the position that to hold otherwise would be a windfall to the tort-feasor, who would then, in effect, escape liability for his own wrongdoing because the plaintiff was fortunate enough or foresighted enough to be provided with protection from another source. These courts reason that if anyone is to have a windfall, it should be the innocent plaintiff and not the wrongdoing defendant.

An additional argument in support of the rule is the fact that in many instances a plaintiff officer who recovers damages from the tort-feasor will be obligated to repay to the employer from the amount recovered any sums paid to the officer by the employer as a result of the injury.[13]

Not all jurisdictions accept the collateral source doctrine. Pennsylvania and Missouri will apparently allow the tort-feasor to reduce the recovery of the plaintiff by whatever amount has been paid to the officer by the employer if the payment by the employer was made as the result of a legal obligation of the employer; Alabama, Colorado, Louisiana, and New York appear to permit any payments made by the employer, whether under legal obligation or gratuitously, to be deducted from the amount recoverable by the plaintiff from the tort-feasor.[14]

B. INJUNCTIVE RELIEF

In certain cases, money damages may not be appropriate or sufficient to accomplish the officer's ends. For example, the officer may be more concerned with preventing future injury than with recovering money damages for a past injury. A typical case might be one in which the officer is being subjected to a campaign of harassment, and wants it stopped. In such event, the officer may go to court and request that the court issue an order directing the defendant to terminate the harassment immediately.

Court orders of this nature are called injunctions. Injunctions may direct the defendant *not* to do something, in which case they are known as prohibitory injunctions, or they may direct that the defendant take some affirmative action, in which case they are called mandatory injunctions.

In either event, failure to obey the court order is punishable by contempt proceedings, which may result in fine or imprisonment of the defendant. The fact that injunctive relief is being sought does not normally preclude the officer from obtaining money damages as well; most courts may grant either or both if circumstances warrant it.[15]

Research to date indicates that injunctive relief has not often been sought by police officers outside of the labor-management context.[16] Some examples of situations in which injunctive relief *might* be appropriate include:

a. Harassment of the officer or the officer's family by obscene or threatening telephone calls, etc.

b. Defamation cases, in which it appears that the defendant will continue to make derogatory statements about the officer if not ordered to cease and desist.

c. Cases in which an individual or organization is openly advocating violence, thereby inciting future disturbances.

d. Cases in which the owner of premises which must be patrolled by police is allowing a condition to exist on the premises which threatens the safety of the officer.

These are intended only as examples, of course. Injunctive relief should be sought in *any* case in which the officer anticipates future injury of any kind if the defendant's behavior is not altered by court order. This remedy may be of particular interest to police associations seeking to protect their members against threatened harm, and the larger the number of persons threatened by that harm, the more likely it is that the court will grant the injunction.[17]

CHAPTER 4 — NOTES

1. BLACK'S LAW DICTIONARY 467 (4th ed. 1951).

2. In actions for infliction of mental distress, mental suffering may be compensated even in the absence of physical injury. *See* Ch. 6 *infra*.

3. *See* Ch. 8 *infra*.

4. *See* Ch. 2 *supra*.

5. For further discussion of compensatory damages, *see* 22 AM. JUR. 2d *Damages* §§ 11-235 (1965).

6. BLACK'S LAW DICTIONARY 467 (4th ed. 1951). *See also* 22 AM. JUR. 2d *Damages* § 243 (1965).

7. For a full discussion of the confusion over punitive damage awards, *see* 22 AM. JUR. 2d *Damages* §§ 241, 242 (1965). Some courts have apparently solved the problem by regarding nominal damages as a form of "actual" damages. See the discussion of nominal damages in the next section.

8. Multimillion dollar punitive damage awards have been obtained against large corporate defendants (*e.g.,* automobile manufacturers).

9. For a further discussion of nominal damages, *see* 22 AM. JUR. 2d *Damages* §§ 5-10 (1965).

10. *Police and Military Persons as Plaintiffs and Defendants,* Jury Verdict Research, Inc., 1974. It should be noted that the bulk of the jury verdicts studied in this sample were based upon injuries suffered in motor vehicle accidents.

11. *Id.*

12. For example, the out-of-court settlements in the sample ranged in amounts from $5.00 to $25,000.00; the trial awards in the sample ranged from $101.00 to $373,839.77.

13. *See* Ch. 3 *supra.*

14. *See* 7 A.L.R.3d 516 (1966).

15. In some states, equitable remedies (of which the injunction is one) must be sought in a separate court or session of court. In most jurisdictions, however, law and equity have been completely merged, and any superior court may issue an injunction.

16. *Cf.* THE POLICE PLAINTIFF, 78-1, at 6. This remedy is more commonly sought in cases related to employment, promotion, discipline, etc.

17. For further discussion of the injunctive remedy, *see* 42 AM. JUR. 2d *Injunctions* (1969).

Part III
SPECIFIC ACTIONS

Chapter 5

ACTIONS FOR PHYSICAL INJURIES TO THE OFFICER'S PERSON

A. INTENTIONAL INJURIES TO THE PERSON

Personal injuries may be classified as intentional or negligent.[1] The specific form of the action and the elements which must be proven are substantially different for the two types. In particular, the state of mind of the defendant at the time of the injurious act is an important factor in determining which type of suit should be filed.

The term "intentional" as used in the law of torts has a special meaning; in tort law, generally speaking, an act is "intentional" not only when the defendant has acted maliciously, or for the *purpose* of causing an injury, but also when the act was done without malice or desire to harm but with *knowledge to a substantial certainty that harm would follow.*[2]

The exact "intent" which must be found varies somewhat, depending upon the specific type of tort action. Consequently, the intent element will be covered separately as part of the discussion of each individual intentional tort action, both in this chapter and elsewhere in the book.

1. *Battery*

a. Definition and Elements.

Battery may be defined as an intentional, unlawful, offensive bodily contact.[3] Each element of this definition has a technical meaning, and each must be proved by the plaintiff officer before there can be a recovery.

(1) *The Contact Must Be Intentional.*

The contact with the officer's person must have been an intentional one; one who bumps into the plaintiff inadvertently is not liable for battery, however clumsy or careless the defendant may have been.[4] It is not necessary, however, that the defendant have intended to cause *injury;* if the *contact itself* was intended, that is sufficient to satisfy the intent element. (Again, however, note that the contact is "intended" if the defendant (a) made the contact deliberately or (b) *acted with knowledge to a substantial certainty that contact would result.*)

(2) *The Contact Must Be Unlawful.*

If the contact was lawful, there is no battery, and certain types of personal contact are permitted by custom or by law. For example, routine minor physical contacts in the course of everyday life, such as brushing against someone while trying to enter or leave a bus, or tapping someone on the shoulder to ask directions, are generally held to be not actionable.

Under certain circumstances even very violent contacts may be held to be privileged. Therefore, if the plaintiff police officer is acting unlawfully at the time, the defendant citizen may be privileged to resist the arrest with some degree of force. (See b(2)(b) *infra.*)

(3) *The Contact Must Be "Offensive."*

The contact must be offensive. This does not mean, however, that the contact must be a violent or painful one. Even the slightest touching of the officer in a rude, angry, or otherwise offensive manner is actionable.[5]

Note that the fact that there is no actual wound or other physical injury is irrelevant to the question of liability; even the lightest contact, if it is offensive, is sufficient to complete the tort, and the presence or absence of resultant pain or physical injury is important only on the question of the damages to be assessed.

94

Further, there need not be actual contact with the body of the officer. One who fires a bullet through an officer's sleeve, or knocks off the officer's hat, or rips off the officer's badge, is liable for battery.[6] Indeed, contact with any object closely associated with the officer's person, such as a radio, belt, holster, nightstick, etc. may be sufficient to constitute battery. The type of weapon used is immaterial. Thus, battery may be committed using firearms, knives, clubs, bottles, fists, feet, or any other portion of the body. A remarkable number of cases involve automobiles.[7]

In addition to the foregoing, certain other aspects of the tort of battery should be kept in mind.

First of all, battery should be carefully distinguished from "assault," which is discussed later in this chapter. Although the term "assault" is often used interchangeably with the term "battery," the two are in fact separate and distinct torts. (See Section 2 *infra.*) Secondly, it should be remembered that the *crime* of battery and the *tort* of battery are two distinct legal actions; the definition of, and rules applicable to, the crime of battery are in many jurisdictions substantially different from those applicable to the tort. The principles discussed here refer to the *tort* of battery as recognized by the common law. The fact that the defendant has also been charged with the *crime* of battery will not prevent the bringing of a tort action. Indeed, the conviction for the crime of battery may be helpful to the officer in the civil action, for a guilty plea or confession in the criminal action may be admissible as a party admission in the civil action, and conviction in the criminal trial may even prevent the defendant from asserting the same defenses in the civil action.[8]

Because battery is an intentional tort, punitive damages are usually available, even where the actual damage is small or nonexistent.[9] The fact that the defendant has incurred

95

penalties for the crime of battery will not preclude the assessment of punitive damages in the tort action.[10]

When the result of the battery is the death of the officer, the action becomes one for wrongful death in most jurisdictions. Wrongful death is a statutory action and is discussed separately below.

The two primary defenses in battery actions are (a) that the plaintiff consented in some manner to the battery (as where the parties mutually agree to step outside and settle an argument with fists), and (b) that the defendant was attacked by the plaintiff first and acted only in self-defense. The former defense is rarely raised in police cases; the latter frequently is. (See below.)

b. Battery Actions by Police Plaintiffs.

(1) *General Considerations.*

Battery may be the tort most often committed against police officers; it is certainly the one about which the most complete statistics are available. According to the FBI's Uniform Crime Reports, there were 49,079 reported physical attacks upon police officers in this country in 1976. Of these, 18,737 resulted in serious injury to the officers involved.[11]

These figures are even more sobering when it is considered that these are only the *reported* attacks; it seems probable that this is only the tip of the iceberg, and that a large number of attacks which do not culminate in major bodily contact are occurring but are not officially reported.

Despite the frequency with which the tort occurs, relatively few actions for battery have been brought by police officers. Although no national statistics are presently available, it is perhaps worth noting that at the time of this writing, of all the civil cases in the author's files in which police officers were plaintiffs, *only 28 percent involved a charge of battery.*[12]

96

Nevertheless, a significant number of battery actions are being brought by police officers, and a significant number of favorable verdicts are being obtained in this particular type of action.[13]

In addition, when favorable results are obtained, the judgments tend to be substantial.[14]

(2) *Special Problems in Battery Actions by Police Plaintiffs.*

As with other tort actions, police officers bringing suit for battery are confronted by certain problems not faced by the ordinary plaintiff. Of these special difficulties perhaps the most formidable is the plea of self-defense so often raised by defendants who have attacked and injured police officers. Many if not most attacks on police officers occur when the officer is attempting to approach, detain, or arrest the defendant, and the two most commonly asserted bases for the self-defense plea in suits by police officers for battery are (a) that the police officer failed to identify himself properly; and (b) that the police officer's own actions were unlawful.

(a) Failure of the Officer to Identify Himself Properly. Defendants frequently contend that they struck the plaintiff officer in self-defense because they did not know that the plaintiff was in fact a police officer, and believed that they themselves were being threatened or attacked by a criminal.[15] Since a reasonable mistake of fact will justify the use of force in self-defense, this is a complete defense to the action if the jury finds that the defendant had no reasonable grounds for knowing that the plaintiff was a law enforcement officer. The defendant usually seeks to establish this by showing (1) that the plaintiff was not in uniform, or that the uniform was not visible, and (2) that the officer failed to identify himself as such when approaching the defendant.

(b) Officer's Own Actions Unlawful. Even if the officer was in proper uniform and/or did identify himself properly

97

to the defendant, the defendant may still escape liability if the officer was otherwise acting improperly or unlawfully at the time the officer was attacked. This may take the form of (1) lack of lawful authority to make the arrest or (2) making a lawful arrest in an unlawful manner.

If the officer is attempting to make an arrest without lawful authority, the person being arrested may be entitled to resist the arrest. This right was recognized at common law, and is accepted by statute or case law in many American jurisdictions.[16] Other jurisdictions have abolished this right by statute or rejected it in case law; [17] in these jurisdictions, there is no right to resist an officer with force even if the arrest is unlawful. This is the position taken by the American Law Institute [18] and is probably the trend today. Furthermore, even in those jurisdictions which permit resistance to lawful arrest, the right to resist is limited to the use of reasonable force; excessive use of force in resisting should not be permitted, even if the arrest is unlawful. Thus, if the defendant has wounded or killed the officer, a right of action for battery should exist in any jurisdiction, for in such cases the defendant has exceeded the scope of the resistance privilege.[19]

(3) *Arrest Made in Unlawful Manner; Use of Excessive Force by Officer.*

Even in jurisdictions where there is no right to resist unlawful arrest, the rule is normally limited to situations where the arrest itself is unlawful for technical reasons, such as lack of a warrant, lack of authority to arrest without a warrant, officer outside of his jurisdiction, etc. *If the officer employs excessive force in effecting the arrest, the defendant may be entitled to resist with like force under the self-defense principle discussed earlier,* and this may be so even if the arrest was technically lawful.[20]

The officer may be aided at the trial by a presumption that his actions were lawful and proper, but this presumption is rebuttable; and if the officer provokes the attack by exceeding his lawful authority, the officer cannot expect to recover against the defendant in a battery action.[21]

(4) *Other Considerations.*

The possibility that other persons besides the actual assailant may be liable for the attack has already been pointed out in Chapter 3. However, two points bear additional emphasis here:

(a) There are currently a number of suits being reported in which a third party — individual or organization — is being sued for *negligence* as the result of the *intentional* act of the actual attacker. This approach appears to offer significant opportunities to the injured officer and is discussed later in this chapter.

(b) The action for battery (or assault and battery) may be useful as a basis for a counterclaim when the officer is himself being sued for using excessive force, etc. The counterclaim strategy is discussed in Chapter 11.

2. *Assault*

It is common to speak of "assault and battery" in the same breath, much as we say "bacon and eggs" or "peanut butter and jelly." This practice tends to obscure the fact that, although assault and battery are indeed closely related, they are in reality two separate torts with distinct elements. To complicate matters, in many jurisdictions it is not uncommon to find the term "assault" being used to describe what is technically the tort of battery.[22] This is both confusing and unfortunate, because although the same incident often gives rise to *both* causes of action, either may exist without the other.

Assault very seldom involves any actual physical injury to the person of the plaintiff. The action is allowed, nevertheless, because an assault is an interference with the sanctity of the person, and it is the policy of the law to discourage such behavior. It is sometimes said that damages are allowed for assault to compensate the plaintiff for fright suffered because of the defendant's behavior, a rationale developed many years ago before the tort of intentional infliction of mental distress was recognized.

Despite the fact that it seldom involves physical injury, it is discussed in this chapter because it is so closely associated in the public mind with battery, so often arises out of the same incident as battery, and is so often brought in the same action as battery.

a. Definition and Elements.

Assault may be defined as "An intentional, unlawful offer of corporal injury to another ... under such circumstances as to create well founded fear of imminent peril, coupled with apparent present ability to execute (the) attempt ...." [23]

These elements will be examined separately.

(1) *The Act Must Be Intentional.*

In this context, intent is found when the defendant deliberately makes a threatening gesture toward the plaintiff either with the intent to accomplish a battery or with the intent to cause the plaintiff to believe that a battery will be accomplished.[24] Thus, for example, if the defendant deliberately points a firearm at the officer for the purpose of shooting or frightening the officer, there is an assault; if the gun is merely carelessly held so that the muzzle is unconsciously pointed in the direction of the officer, no assault has occurred.

100

(2) *The Act Must Be Unlawful.*

As with battery, the act is not tortious if done with legal justification or excuse. The privilege of self-defense, for example, would excuse what would otherwise be an assault.[25]

(3) *There Must Be an "Offer of Injury."*

Plaintiff must show that there was an *overt gesture* by defendant ("offer") which conveyed to the planitiff the threat of battery. *Words alone are not enough to constitute an assault.* However, an ambiguous gesture may be rendered sufficiently threatening to constitute assault if accompanied by ominous words; conversely, a gesture which might otherwise in itself constitute assault may be rendered legally harmless by accompanying statements which clearly indicate that no assault is intended.[26]

(4) *The Gesture Must Create an Apprehension of Immediate Battery.*

The gesture, together with any accompanying words, must create the belief that battery is imminent. Threats of future harm, while they may be actionable under statute or other common-law forms of action,[27] are not assault. Here again, words may *prevent* an otherwise threatening gesture from being assault, if they indicate that no *immediate* harm is planned.[28]

Note that actual *fear* is not required. The term "apprehension" is used because actual fear or fright is not essential. The *expectation* of immediate battery is enough for assault, even though the plaintiff is not actually *afraid* of the consequences.

(5) *The Apprehension Must Be Reasonable.*

No amount of apprehension, even when it amounts to real fear, is sufficient unless the apprehension was reasonable. Phobias or other illogical or unreasonable reactions are not sufficient. Whether the apprehension is reasonable depends in part on the next requirement:

(6) *The Defendant Must Have Apparent Ability to Complete the Battery.*

Note that liability does not depend upon the *actual* intent or *actual* ability of the assailant to injure the officer. What counts is *apparent* intent and ability. Consequently, even where the assailant points an unloaded gun at the officer, or points a gun (whether loaded or unloaded) solely to frighten the officer and with no actual intent to fire it, the officer still has an action for assault.[29]

Note that no physical contact of any kind is required for assault. Note also that there need be no actual injury of any kind.[30] If there *is* some actual damage, as, for example, where a startled officer jumps back, trips, falls, and suffers harm, or is so frightened that severe mental anguish results, that will of course increase the damage award. But no actual injury need be shown; nominal damages may be awarded, and, in addition, punitive damages may be available.[31]

b. Actions for Assault by Police Plaintiffs.

Many actions are brought by officers for "assault *and* battery," but apparently very few are brought for assault alone. Presumably this is because assault alone, unaccompanied by physical contact, seldom involves significant actual damage, and officers are therefore not sufficiently interested to bring action for it.

Nevertheless, numerous true assaults may occur in the line of duty. The angry man who shakes his fist; the drunk who swings and misses; the suspect who pulls a knife or a gun; and the demonstrator who hurls a rock are all liable for assault, even where no physical contact is made. (Indeed, the difference between assault and battery may be only a matter

102

of bad aim; to fire at the officer and *miss* is assault; to fire at and *hit* the officer is battery.) Yet, as noted, officers seldom sue for assault when there has been no battery, even though the difference between fright and injury — or life and death — may be a matter of a fraction of an inch.

An assault action by a police officer would be subject to the same problems discussed above in connection with battery; the self-defense justification would be available where the officer has not clearly indentified himself as such, or has acted without proper authority or with excessive force.

Despite the lack of assault actions, officers should bear in mind the existence of the right. Where actual harm has occurred, or where matters of principle or example are involved, the action is available.

B. NEGLIGENT INJURIES

1. *General Negligence Principles*

The general principles of negligence actions are easily stated, although practical application is sometimes difficult. Broadly speaking, all of us owe to other persons a duty to use reasonable care to avoid injuring them in the course of our activities. If we fail to use such care, and that failure causes injury to another person, that person has a right of action against us. To recover in a negligence suit, then, the plaintiff must show (1) that the defendant owed to the plaintiff a *duty of due care;* (2) that defendant *breached that duty;* and (3) that the breach of duty by the defendant was the *cause* of (4) *actual damage* to the plaintiff.

a. Duty of Due Care.

There is a general duty to avoid injury to others. This duty is owed to virtually everyone (there are a few exceptions where the duty is limited — *e.g.,* assailants and trespassers)

103

and requires that all of us act in any given situation as an "ordinary prudent person" or "reasonable man" would act in that situation. Generally speaking, this mythical "ordinary prudent person" will not do, or fail to do, any act if it is "foreseeable" that that act or omission to act will cause harm to others.

b. Breach of Duty of Due Care.

If the defendant has breached this duty of due care, *i.e.,* has failed to behave as the ordinary prudent person would behave under the same circumstances, the defendant has been "negligent." This does not necessarily mean that the defendant is *liable* for money damages, because the remaining elements of the tort we call "negligence" must be satisfied.

c. Causation.

To be actionable, the defendant's negligence must have been the *cause* of the plaintiff's injury. Proof of causation can be difficult, because whereas a layman might say that the defendant "caused" the injury, the law may refuse to recognize causation because the act of the defendant is so far removed from the eventual injury to the plaintiff that it is not fair or practical to hold the defendant responsible for the ultimate harm. Thus "causation in fact" is not enough; *legal* causation (usually called "*proximate* cause") must be found. Thus, for example, the chain of events leading from the defendant's act to the eventual injury to the plaintiff may be so long or so unusual that the court will simply refuse to hold the defendant liable, even though in fact defendant may have triggered the series of events which eventually led to the injury.

d. Damages.

Finally, *there must be some actual damage* to the plaintiff. Nominal damages cannot be awarded in negligence actions;

there is no liability at all unless the plaintiff has suffered actual injury in some degree, however small.

There are degrees of negligence, ranging today from "simple negligence" through "gross negligence" to "reckless" (or "willful and wanton") conduct. Where the defendant has behaved recklessly or wantonly, punitive damages are available, provided that there is some actual damage. (Again, in negligence, unlike the intentional tort actions, if there is no actual damage there is no liability and, indeed, no cause of action at all.)

There are certain defenses to negligence actions; most important is the rule that if the plaintiff has contributed to his own injury, plaintiff cannot recover or, in some jurisdictions, can recover only a reduced amount. Thus, if the *plaintiff* has been careless, and this carelessness has contributed to the injury,[32] or if plaintiff has knowingly entered the area of danger, thereby deliberately exposing himself to the risk of injury,[33] defendant may avoid liability, or may have to pay for only a part of the plaintiff's damages.

Negligence actions arise from rights developed under the common law. If the negligent act of the defendant results in the death of the plaintiff, the action is normally brought under a specific state statute as a "wrongful death" action. Wrongful death actions are discussed later in this chapter.

2. Negligence Actions by Police Officers

Although much interest is currently being taken in intentional injuries to police officers, due to the relatively greater increase in the number of intentional injuries and the broader issues of lawlessness and deterrence involved, it is a simple fact that a great many officers are hurt in the line of duty by the unintentional carelessness of those who are commonly called "decent citizens."

Traditionally, however, there have been proportionately even fewer actions by police officers for negligent injuries than for intentional injuries. This is due in part to the existence of the workmen's compensation and medical insurance plans which cover most law enforcement personnel, and perhaps in part to the fact that negligent injuries may arouse less anger than intentional ones.[34] The officer injured by the negligence of another person typically receives compensation directly through the employing law enforcement agency's workmen's compensation plan, and returns to duty without further legal involvement. This need not always be the result, however. Two points discussed earlier bear repeating here: (1) Acceptance of workmen's compensation or hospitalization benefits does not necessarily deprive the officer of a right of action against the person or persons who caused the injury, and (2) the recovery in a common-law negligence action will frequently far exceed the total of any possible benefits payable under workmen's compensation or medical insurance plans.[35]

There has been little if any organized attempt by police associations to encourage the filing of negligence actions. These campaigns are, of course, motivated primarily by a desire to deter intentional wrongs, such as battery or defamation. It is doubtful that negligence actions have much (if any) deterrent effect upon future carelessness. Nevertheless, the financial impact of a given injury is the same whether the defendant acted deliberately or merely carelessly, and police officers should be aware of their rights in negligence actions.

a. Negligence Actions by Police Plaintiffs Generally.

Generally speaking, police officers have the same rights of recovery for injuries caused to them by the negligence of others that are enjoyed by all citizens. Therefore, the police officer who is injured by the carelessness of another person may normally recover compensation in a negligence action to the same extent, and subject to the same defenses, as any other plaintiff. These general principles of negligence will therefore not be considered further here.[36]

b. Specific Types of Negligence Actions by Police Plaintiffs.

There are, however, three specific types of negligence actions which are of special interest to police officers. Because of the nature of police work, many negligent injuries occur in these particular contexts, and the bulk of reported negligence actions being brought by police officers appear to fall into one of these three categories.[37] The categories are (1) motor vehicle injuries; (2) injuries due to physical defects on the property of citizens (premises defects); and (3) injuries *intentionally* caused by a third person for which the present defendant may be liable due to defendant's own negligence.

(1) *Motor Vehicle Injuries.*

(a) Generally. Because most police officers spend a significant amount of time literally "on the street," they are exposed to numerous vehicular hazards. Officers have been injured by motor vehicles in numerous situations, both while in vehicles [38] and while on foot.[39]

For the most part, officers involved in motor vehicle accidents enjoy the same rights granted to any other plaintiff. For example, they may prove the negligence of the defendant by showing that the defendant was, at the time of the collision, violating a traffic law,[40] and they may hold an employer liabile for the negligence of an employee driving an automobile within the scope of the employment.[41] On the other hand, as in other types of cases, the officer's own employer may be able to recover some portion of the award from the officer if benefits have been paid.[42]

(b) Suits for Injuries Suffered While in Pursuit of the Defendant. Officers have been able to recover in several instances for injuries suffered in motor vehicle accidents which occurred while the plaintiff officer was in pursuit of the defendant's vehicle, even though the defendant's vehicle was not directly involved in the accident. When the defendant unlawfully attempts to evade the pursuing officer, it is foreseeable that injury to the officer may result, and such behavior by the defendant is held to be negligence *per se* and the proximate cause of the officer's injury.[43]

(c) Defenses in Motor Vehicle Cases. As with any negligence case, contributory negligence of the plaintiff is a partial or complete defense to the action. The mere act of pursuit is not contributory negligence, since the officer is under a duty to pursue; but if the chase is conducted negligently and/or in violation of statute or ordinance, the officer driving the police car may be found negligent.[44]

It has been held that the negligence, if any, of an officer/driver is not imputed to an officer/passenger in the same patrol car, and that the officer/passenger's failure to use the radio to warn other pursuing police cars of the location of the officer/passenger's vehicle is not contributory negligence on the part of the officer/passenger.[45]

(2) *Premises Defects.*

(a) Generally. Many officers are injured by physical defects on premises which they enter in the line of duty. In the past, such officers have had great difficulty in recovering against the owner (or possessor) of the premises because of the rules of law which limit the duty owed to them by the premises owners.

Traditionally, a person who enters the premises of another has been categorized by the law either as a trespasser, a licensee, or an invitee. A trespasser is one who enters without any right to do so; a licensee is one who enters with the permission of the premises owner, whether express or implied, or under some right granted by law or custom irrespective of consent; an invitee, sometimes called a business invitee or business visitor, is one who enters the premises for the pecuniary benefit of the premises owner or for the express purpose for which the premises are held open to the public by the owner. (For example, a customer entering a retail store is usually an invitee.)

The significance of these categories is that when a person is injured on the premises by a defect in the premises, the owner's liability to the injured person will be determined by the classification of the injured person as a trespasser, licensee, or invitee.

There is virtually no duty on the part of the premises owner toward the undiscovered trespasser; this category is seldom involved in police cases and will not be discussed further here. The important categories for purposes of this discussion are licensee and invitee.

The premises owner owes no duty to a licensee to repair defects; the owner need only warn the licensee of hidden defects which the owner knows the licensee is likely to encounter, and that duty can arise only when the owner knows that the licensee will be entering the premises and the particular portion thereof where the defect is located. Where there is no duty, there can of course be no breach of duty, and therefore no negligence and no liability. Licensees therefore often encounter great difficulty in recovering for premises injuries.

An invitee, by contrast, has an excellent chance of recovery for injury caused by premises defects, because the premises owner owes to the invitee a positive duty to keep the premises safe; the owner must inspect for defects and make the necessary repairs to protect the invitee from injury.

It is therefore of the utmost importance to determine the category applicable to the plaintiff in a premises injury case.

(b) Premises Defect Actions by Police Plaintiffs. Unfortunately, courts have traditionally placed firemen and police officers in the category of licensees, meaning that only the very limited duty described above is owed to the police officer (or fireman) who is injured on the premises in the line of duty.[46] As a result, earlier cases brought by police officers for premises injuries usually ended in defeat for the injured officer, and many states still follow the licensee rule.[47]

Some states, feeling that police and firefighters do not fit into any of the traditional categories because they usually enter premises not with consent or as customers but as a matter of legal right and public duty, have classified police officers and firemen as *sui generis,* meaning simply "in a class by themselves." These *sui generis* states have, however, generally imposed upon the premises owner as to this separate class only the same limited duty that is owed to licensees — that is, the owner is liable for premises defects only if the owner (1) knows of the presence of the officer, (2) knows of the dangerous condition, and (3) knows or has reason to know that the officer is unaware of and will not discover the defect. Thus, these *"sui generis"* jurisdictions have also severely limited the police officer's right of recovery for premises defects.[48]

The rather unfavorable treatment accorded to firefighters and police officers in this area of the law has apparently been based in part upon the almost universal availability of employee compensation plans to cover the cost of injuries, and in part upon the view that these public servants assume the risks inherent in their respective occupations. This attitude is manifested in many jurisdictions by adoption of the so-called "fireman's rule," which holds that a fireman who is injured in fighting a fire may not recover damages for the injuries from the person whose negligence caused the fire.[49] Although called the "fireman's" rule, the rule is often applied to police officers as well.[50] The rule has certain limitations. For example, it usually applies only to *paid* personnel injured by the *passive* negligence of the defendant in allowing the fire to start.[51] The owner or occupant of the premises remains liable for "... failure to warn of unusual or hidden hazards, for actively negligent conduct and, in some jurisdictions, for statutory violations creating undue risks of injury ...." [52]

Because of these qualifications to the fireman's rule, the result of a given case will usually be the same whether the court relies expressly on the fireman's rule or merely treats the plaintiff as a licensee under the principles described earlier herein. Many decisions which expressly label the plaintiff as "licensee" or "*sui generis*" are, in fact, applying the fireman's rule.[53]

Thus, whether the jurisdiction has expressly adopted the fireman's rule or not, the police officer often faces formidable obstacles in cases of this nature.

This does *not* mean that the plaintiff police officer cannot ever succeed in such actions, however. Even the strict rules discussed above have qualifications and exceptions, and, in addition, many courts have become dissatisfied with the old rules and have sought to find better solutions to the problem. Thus, depending upon the jurisdiction, the court may permit a recovery under one or more of the following theories:

(i) The court may simply declare that police officers are invitees. As noted above, premises owners owe invitees a duty to make the premises safe, and failure to do so is negligence. If the officer is declared to be an invitee, therefore, the chances of recovery are greatly multiplied.[54]

(ii) In many instances, the courts have held that while policemen are not necessarily invitees in all cases, they *may* be invitees in a particular case, and have looked to the facts of the case to determine if the officer will be treated as a licensee or invitee in that particular instance. These courts have used one or both of two methods of determining the status of the officer:

111

(1) the reason for the officer's presence on the premises, and/or

(2) the portion of the premises where the injury occurred.

Under the first approach, if the officer is on the premises *at the request of the premises owner* (*e.g.,* in response to a call for help) *or for the benefit of the owner* (*e.g.,* checking for intruders) the officer is an *invitee;* if on the premises for other purposes, he is a licensee.[55]

Under the second approach, if at the time of the injury the plaintiff officer was in a portion of the premises normally open to the public, the officer is an invitee; if in other areas, a licensee. The time of day — during business hours or after the premises have been closed to the public — seems to be relevant here also.[56]

(iii) Some courts have rejected the old licensee-invitee labels entirely and measured the duty of the premises owner by the standard of reasonableness. Thus, the owner must take such measures to protect police officers entering the premises as are reasonable under the circumstances. Since this approach often produces the same result that would have been obtained under the old licensee-invitee rules, it may not greatly improve the officer's position; but at least it is potentially more flexible than the older rule.[57]

(iv) In some cases courts have ruled that, although the officer was merely a licensee (or was subject to the "fireman's rule"), *under the circumstances of the case* the premises owner was obligated to give the police officer notice of the defect, thereby making the owner liable for failure to give the notice.

Thus, it is often held that even though the premises owner has only the limited duty owed to a licensee to warn of hidden defects, the premises owner is liable for failure to warn the fireman or police officer if the premises owner actually knows the fireman or officer is on the premises [58] *or has reason to anticipate* the presence of the officer.[59] This last argument appears to be of particular interest to police plaintiffs in states which retain the limited duty, and counsel should always determine if the premises owner had any notice that officers were or would be entering the premises. Even when the officer is a licensee, the premises owner must warn the officer of known hidden defects *if the owner has opportunity to do so.* (Although this is not an actual departure from older law but merely a question of interpretation of the facts, it often appears that courts which reach this result are really dissatisfied with the old rule and wish to mitigate its harshness.)

It should be noted that even where the police officer has been declared to be an invitee or the equivalent, there is no duty on the part of the premises owner to protect the officer from *obvious dangers,* and the contributory negligence of the officer is still a defense to the action.[60]

The liability of premises owners to police officers injured by defects on the premises is one of the few areas of police plaintiff litigation in which there is a substantial body of case precedent available. Because of the differences in the rules in the various states, plaintiff and counsel should consult the appellate opinions of the particular jurisdiction.[61]

(3) *Recovery for Negligence of the Premises Owner Leading to Intentional Injury by a Third Person.*

The preceding discussion related primarily to those injuries which arise from physical defects in the premises themselves. A different question is presented when an officer enters premises and is there injured by the intentional act of some third person also present on the premises. Of course, the actual assailant is liable — if he or she can be found — and this liability is covered in the discusssions in this chapter of battery and wrongful death. The issue now under examination is whether the *owner of the premises* may be held liable for the assailant's act.

Several cases have been brought by officers on the theory that the negligence of the owner of the premises was a causal factor in the officer's injury by a third person. The major difficulty in such suits results from the general principle of tort law that when an *intentional criminal act* intervenes between the negligence of the defendant and the injury to the plaintiff, that intentional act is a "superseding cause" of the injury and relieves the negligent defendant from liability, even though the defendant's negligence created the conditions which made the criminal act possible. The usual explanation for this rule is that the defendant cannot be expected to anticipate the criminal acts of other persons.[62]

This principle has been applied to defeat actions by injured officers against premises owners.[63]

Again, however, as a matter of general tort law, if the defendant *should have foreseen* that an intentional intervening act might precipitate injury, the defendant will be liable for any negligence which contributed to the ultimate result. This qualification to the general rule of non-liability has resulted in at least one favorable verdict for the injured officer. In a recent case, an Illinois appellate court, affirming a verdict for an officer shot on the defendant's premises, said:

> The act of a third person in committing an intentional tort or crime is a superseding cause of harm to another resulting therefrom, although the actor's negligent conduct created a situation which afforded an opportunity to the third person to commit such a tort or crime, *unless the actor at the time of his negligent conduct realized or should have realized* the likelihood that such a situation might be created, and that a third person might avail himself of the opportunity to commit such a tort or crime.[64]

It appears that the injured officer must therefore show that the premises owner *should have foreseen* that the owner's negligence might lead to a criminal attack upon the officer.

Even this may not be enough, however. Despite the fact that the criminal conduct was foreseeable to the negligent premises owner, the officer may be barred from recovery *if the danger of criminal conduct was obvious to the officer.* Thus, when an officer was shot by burglars while checking an unlighted area on the defendant's premises, the court denied recovery against the premises owner on the grounds that, irrespective of the question of the owner's negligence, "the fact that the property was not illuminated was obvious to all." [65]

It therefore appears that in some jurisdictions, recoveries will be possible only when (a) the intervening criminal conduct was foreseeable by the defendant and (b) the danger was not obvious to the plaintiff. In addition, some states will apply the so-called "fireman's rule," which prevents firemen and police officers from recovering for the negligence which brought them to the scene to begin with. Thus, in a 1977 California case, a police officer who was attacked and injured when he attempted to arrest a drunk at a party in a private home was denied recovery against the owners of the home, despite the fact that liquor was being served to minors on the premises in violation of a statute.[66]

In states following this approach, the officer's chances of success are severely reduced, although it still may be possible to recover by showing some negligence on the part of the premises owner *after* the officer arrived on the scene.

C. WRONGFUL DEATH

When the injury to the person of the police officer proves to be fatal, the action is usually not labeled "battery" or

115

"negligence," but is brought as an action for "wrongful death." These actions are governed by statute,[67] and the exact procedures and concepts involved therefore vary from jurisdiction to jurisdiction. Certain characteristics or principles common to most such statutes are:

(1) The right of action is usually considered to belong to the surviving family members, rather than to the deceased officer.[68] However, the actual plaintiff in the action may, depending upon the particular statute, be either a surviving family member or the deceased officer's "personal representative," by which is meant either the person named in the officer's will as executor of the will, if there is one, or, if there is not a will, a person (usually called an "administrator") appointed by the court to administer the deceased officer's affairs and see to the distribution of the officer's property to the surviving relatives.[69]

(2) Any recovery obtained in the wrongful death action goes to the surviving family members after the deceased's expenses (*e.g.,* hospital and funeral bills) have been paid. Normally, if the officer leaves behind a spouse or child, the recovery will go to the spouse and/or child; if there is no spouse or child, other relatives, such as brothers or sisters, parents, etc. will receive the award.[70]

(3) Although the right of action is said to belong to the survivors, and not to the deceased officer, *any defense which could have been asserted against the officer may be asserted by the defendant against the person bringing the wrongful death action.* Thus, for example, if it should be determined at the trial that the officer was himself at fault, and that this improper conduct on the part of the officer contributed to his death, the survivors might be barred from recovery, or their recovery might be reduced in proportion to the degree of the officer's fault.

Despite the fact that they are governed by statute and called by a different name, wrongful death actions involve the same basic principles of liability as those found in actions in which the plaintiff is only injured. Thus, for example, where a battery has been committed which has resulted in death, the deceased's survivors must establish in court the elements of battery, and the case is subject to the same defenses as those available in a battery action. If the death was due to negligence, the elements of negligence must be shown, and the same defenses apply. The main effect of the wrongful death statutes, therefore, is to permit the right of action to survive the deceased person, and, in some instances, to govern the nature, extent, and distribution of the recovery, if any. Otherwise, wrongful death actions are basically the same as personal injury actions, and the same elements must be proven for liability to be found.[71]

D. PRODUCTS LIABILITY

When a product causes injury to the user, the manufacturer (and wholesaler and retailer) may be held liable for the injury. Thus, for example, if a handgun is manufactured with a flawed barrel, and in normal service use blows up because of the defect and injures the officer firing the weapon, the manufacturer may be liable.

This liability may be based on improper design or improper manufacture, and the action may be for negligence, breach of express or implied warranty, or, in many jurisdictions, for strict liability.

Most product liability suits involve direct injuries to the plaintiff by the product itself. A more difficult question is presented when a product (such as a handgun) is being utilized in self-defense and the failure of the product does not itself directly injure the user but leaves the user defenseless against a criminal attack which causes injury.

117

Obviously it would be advantageous for economic reasons for an officer injured under these circumstances to be able to hold the manufacturer liable for the failure, but the problem of superseding cause, discussed in connection with premises owners (above) will apply in this situation as well.

Nevertheless, at least one case of this type has resulted in a recovery; the defense of superseding cause was rejected and judgment for the plaintiff affirmed.[72] Although the plaintiff in the case was a motel clerk and not a police officer, the same principle would seem to apply in police plaintiff cases.

Therefore, in any instance in which an item of equipment has failed to perform a *defensive function* properly and the officer has been injured in the resulting attack, a products liability action against the manufacturer (and possibly others in the chain of distribution) may be in order.[73]

If the action is brought as a negligence action, it must be established that the manufacturer *should have foreseen* that the failure of the handgun or other defensive device involved would leave the officer vulnerable to criminal attack. Slightly different elements may be involved if the action is based on breach of warranty or strict liability, but the plaintiff's basic point will remain the same — that the defendant *should have realized that if the device failed to perform as represented, the user would suffer harm.*[74]

CHAPTER 5 — NOTES

1. In some jurisdictions, defendants will be held "strictly liable" for certain injuries, meaning that they are liable although they did not intend any harm and were acting with due care at the time of the injury. *See* Products Liability *infra.*

2. *See* PROSSER, LAW OF TORTS § 8 (4th ed. 1971).

3. *See* BLACK'S LAW DICTIONARY 193 (4th ed. 1951), for further definitions. For further coverage of general principles of battery, *see* PROSSER, LAW OF TORTS § 9 (4th ed. 1971); and 6 AM. JUR. 2d *Assault and Battery* (1963).

4. The defendant may, however, be liable for *negligence* if injury results. *See* Section B below.

5. Touching, tapping, or poking the plaintiff is sufficient; spitting on the plaintiff or throwing dirt, water, excrement, etc., on him could likewise constitute battery. Touching a woman "in an indecent manner" has frequently been held to be battery, a rule which would presumably apply to female police officers.

6. *See, e.g.,* Keane v. Main, 83 Conn. 200, 76 A. 269 (1910) (ripped off badge).

7. *See, e.g.,* Patterson v. Ward, 61 So.2d 595 (La. App. 1952) (fists); Ryan v. Quinn, 24 Ky. 1513, 71 S.W. 872 (Ky. App. 1903) (feet); Tabb v. Norred, 277 So.2d 223 (La. App. 1973) (firearms); Ingram v. Higgins, 103 Cal. App. 2d 287, 229 P.2d 385 (1951) (wine bottle, automobile); Mooney v. Carter, 114 Colo. 267, 160 P.2d 390 (1945) (automobile).

8. Roshak v. Leathers, 277 Ore. 207, 560 P.2d 275 (1977). This rule of "collateral estoppel" may not be asserted in all jurisdictions because of the differences in parties, etc., between the civil and criminal litigations.

9. *See, e.g.,* Smith v. Hubbard, 253 Minn. 215, 91 N.W.2d 756 (1958) (no physical injury, $2,500 punitive damages). *See also* Ch. 4 *supra.*

10. Roshak v. Leathers, 277 Ore. 207, 560 P.2d 275 (1977).

11. FBI *Uniform Crime Reports* Table 68, at 281 (1976). Note the *Uniform Crime Reports* use the term "assault." The Reports appear to be using this term in reference to attacks that actually culminated in a battery, however.

12. This is not offered as a statistically reliable sample. It does indicate a pattern, which appears to be verified by the author's empirical investigations. For example, Houston Police Department records indicate that there were 688 physical attacks on Houston police officers during 1976. Yet inquiry by the writer, which included interviews with police officials, local attorneys, and officers of the local police association,

indicated that no more than a half dozen lawsuits were filed against assailants by Houston police officers during that year.

13. While the sample is too small to be reliable, analysis of cases in the author's files as of this writing revealed that verdicts favoring the plaintiff police officer were obtained in 81% of the reported battery actions. This contrasts favorably with the reported national average of 63% for all types of police plaintiff cases. (*See* Ch. 4 *supra.*)

14. The average award per officer in successful battery cases noted in the author's files at the time of this writing was $55,173.93. This exceeded the average award in known negligence cases, possibly due in part to the availability of punitive damages in intentional tort actions. Again, however, the sample is too small to be considered statistically reliable.

15. *See, e.g.,* Mooney v. Carter, 114 Colo. 267, 160 P.2d 390 (1945), in which the defendant claimed that she intentionally caused the plaintiff, a plainclothes police officer, to fall from the running board of her car because she feared that he was a degenerate or was trying to harm her or her child. The case is cited and discussed in Blunt, *The Battered Policeman,* FBI LAW ENFORCEMENT BULL., Sept. 1974, an excellent article on the subject of battery actions by law enforcement officers.

16. *See, e.g.,* White v. Morris, 345 So.2d 461 (La. 1977).

17. California, Delaware, Illinois, New Hampshire, New York, and Rhode Island, for example, have eliminated the right by statute; the Superior Court of New Jersey has rejected the right to resist unlawful arrest as "no longer necessary because of the legal remedies available." (State v. Koonce, 89 N.J. Super. 169, 184, 214 A.2d 428, 436 (App. Div. 1965).)

18. ALI MODEL PENAL CODE § 3.04(2)(a).

19. *See generally* Chevigny, *The Right to Resist an Unlawful Arrest,* 78 YALE L.J. 1128 (1969).

20. Even if the use of excessive force by the officer does not excuse the defendant in the eyes of the law, it will often do so in the eyes of the jury. Jurors are unlikely to return a favorable or substantial verdict where the officer has used excessive force in overcoming the arrestee.

21. Veillon v. Sylvester, 174 So.2d 189 (La. App. 1965). *See generally* Blunt, *The Battered Policeman,* FBI LAW ENFORCEMENT BULL., Sept. 1974.

22. This is also the practice in the FBI *Uniform Crime Reports,* and appears to be common usage among law enforcement personnel.

23. BLACK'S LAW DICTIONARY 147 (4th ed. 1951).

24. Or with "knowledge to a substantial certainty" that such belief will result. *See* earlier discussion of Intent.

25. *See* the discussion of Self-Defense in connection with Battery, above.

26. For example, if defendant suddenly reaches for something under his coat, liability for assault may depend upon whether he says "I'll blast you" or "Pardon me, I have to get out my handkerchief to blow my nose."

27. *E.g.,* action for mental distress or extortion.

28. For example, showing the plaintiff a set of brass knuckles and saying "If you don't mind your own business, we're going to come back and beat you up," is probably not assault, because the words indicate a threat of future, not immediate, harm.

29. For a complete discussion, *see* PROSSER, LAW OF TORTS § 10 (4th ed. 1971); and 6 AM. JUR. 2d *Assault & Battery* (1963).

30. Tort law imposes liability for assault as part of the general principle that the person is sacred and no unwarranted violation of or interference with the person will be tolerated. Therefore, assault is actionable even though no actual damage is done.

31. Since the same act of the defendant so often includes both an assault and a battery, the actions are frequently joined and damages asked for the combined effect of the two torts.

32. This is called "contributory negligence."

33. This is called "assumption of risk."

34. Of the cases contained in the author's files, only 30.3% were identifiable as negligence actions.

35. *See* Ch. 2 *supra.* Recoveries in police plaintiff negligence actions listed in the author's files at the time of this writing averaged $39,097.20 per officer. The sample is too small to be considered statistically reliable, and individual recoveries may range from a few hundred dollars to several hundred thousand dollars — or more — depending on the circumstances.

36. For further coverage of general negligence principles, *see* PROSSER, LAW OF TORTS Chs. 5-12 (4th ed. 1971); and 58 AM. JUR. 2d *Negligence* (1971).

37. The categories overlap to some extent, so that a particular suit might fall into two, or even all three, of the categories. Of the negligence cases in the author's files at the time of this writing, *over 90% fell into one or more of the three classifications.*

38. As in, *e.g.,* Pitcher v. Kniss, 10 Cal. App. 3d 931, 89 Cal. Rptr. 676 (1970) (sitting in parked vehicle operating radar, struck from rear, verdict $80,000). *See also* cases cited in notes 40 and 42-45 *infra.*

39. As in, *e.g.,* Cooney v. Hughes, 310 Ill. App. 371, 34 N.E.2d 566 (1941) ($3,500) (directing traffic at intersection); and Hinman v. Westinghouse Elec. Co., 88 Cal. App. 188, 471 P.2d 988 (1970) ($120,000) (out of vehicle inspecting roadside hazard).

40. MacDonald v. Hall, 244 A.2d 809 (Me. 1968) (proof of speed law violation raised presumption of negligence); Burgard v. Eff, 1 Ohio App. 2d 483, 205 N.E.2d 400 (1965) (violation of law was negligence *per se*).

41. As in Hinman v. Westinghouse Elec. Co., 88 Cal. Rptr. 188, 471 P.2d 988 (1970).

42. Sullivan v. Sudiak, 30 Ill. App. 3d 899, 333 N.E.2d 60 (1975).

43. *See* Burgard v. Eff, 1 Ohio App. 2d 483, 30 Ohio Op. 2d 503, 205 N.E.2d 400 (1965), (police car went out of control and struck tree); MacDonald v. Hall, 244 A.2d 809 (Me. 1968) (police car left road and overturned); Rhea v. Green, 29 Colo. App. 19, 476 P.2d 760 (1970) (two police vehicles collided during chase); Brechtel v. Lopez, 140 So.2d 189 (La. App. 1962) (police car went out of control and struck utility pole). *See also* McKay v. Hargis, 351 Mich. 409, 88 N.W.2d 456 (1958); Goddard v. Williams, 251 N.C. 128, 110 S.E.2d 820 (1959) (reversed on other grounds); Martin v. Rossignol, 226 Md. 363, 174 A.2d 149 (1961); City of St. Petersburg v. Shannon, 156 So.2d 870 (Fla. App. 1963). *See generally* Note, 21 SYRACUSE L. REV. 224 (1969).

44. The fact that the officer was speeding does not *per se* constitute contributory negligence. Goddard v. Williams, note 43 *supra.* However, the officer must conduct the chase with "that care which a reasonably prudent man would exercise in the discharge of official duties of like nature under like circumstances." McKay v. Hargis, note 43 *supra. See also* Burgard v. Eff, note 3 *supra* (due to failure to sound siren, officer not exempted from speed laws, but violation *not* negligence as a matter of law).

45. Rhea v. Green, note 3 *supra.*

46. If the officer entered the premises in the officer's private capacity — *e.g.,* as a customer and not in the line of duty — the officer would, of course, be an invitee.

47. *See, e.g.,* Sherman v. Suburban Trust Co., 282 Md. 238, 384 A.2d 76 (1978); Scheuner v. Trustees, 175 Ohio St. 163, 192 N.E.2d 38 (1963). *See generally* PROSSER, LAW OF TORTS § 61 (4th ed. 1971); and RESTATEMENT (SECOND) OF TORTS § 345(2).

48. *See, e.g.,* McGee v. Adams Paper & Twine Co., 26 App. Div. 2d 186, 271 N.Y.S.2d 698 (1966); Buren v. Midwest Indus., Inc., 380 S.W.2d 96 (Ky. App. 1964). *But see* Scurti v. City of New York, note 53 *infra,* and accompanying text.

49. *See, e.g.,* McGee v. Adams, note 48 *supra;* Buren v. Midwest Indus., Inc., note 48 *supra;* Giorgi v. Pacific Gas & Elec. Co., 266 Cal. App. 2d 355, 72 Cal. Rptr. 119 (1968). The rule may extend to off-premises injuries as well. *See* Whitten v. Miami-Dade Water & Sewer Auth., 357 So.2d 430 (Fla. App. 1978).

50. *See, e.g.,* Walters v. Sloan, 142 Cal. Rptr. 152, 571 P.2d 609 (1977). *See also* the feature article in THE POLICE PLAINTIFF, 76-3, at 11.

51. McGee v. Adams, note 48 *supra;* Giorgi v. Pacific Gas & Elec. Co., note 49 *supra.*

52. Buren v. Midwest Indus., Inc., 380 S.W.2d 96, 97 (Ky. App. 1964). *See also* Bartholomew v. Klingler Co., 53 Cal. App. 3d 975, 126 Cal. Rptr. 191 (1975) (police officer not barred from recovery by fireman's rule where there was a known, hidden danger and defendant failed to warn plaintiff).

53. *E.g.,* Buren v. Midwest Indus., Inc., note 52 *supra* ("sui generis").

54. Illinois has done this. *See* Dini v. Naiditch, 20 Ill. 2d 406, 170 N.E.2d 881 (1960).

55. *Compare* Cameron v. Abatiell, 127 Vt. 111, 241 A.2d 310 (1968) (invitee) *with* Cook v. Demetrakas, 108 R.I. 397, 275 A.2d 919 (1971) (licensee under facts but Cameron v. Abatiell cited with approval). *See also* Hall v. Holton, 330 So.2d 81 (Fla. App. 1976) (dictum).

56. *See* Nared v. School Dist. of Omaha, 191 Neb. 376, 215 N.W.2d 115 (1974) (officer in attic after business hours — held licensee); and Skupeen v. City of New York, 29 App. Div. 2d 292, 287 N.Y.S.2d 596 (1968).

57. States rejecting the old rules and adopting the reasonableness test include California, Colorado, and, quite recently, apparently New York. *See, e.g.,* Bartholomew v. Klingler Co., 53 Cal. App. 3d 975, 126 Cal. Rptr. 191 (1975); Mile High Fence Co. v. Radovich, 175 Colo. 537, 489 P.2d 308 (1971); and Scurti v. City of New York, 387 N.Y.S.2d 55, 354 N.E.2d 794 (1976) (not a police plaintiff case, but rejects "the ancient and antiquated distinctions between trespassers and licensees" and adopts the "reasonableness standard" for New York). *N.B.:* Adoption of the reasonableness test does not preclude application of the fireman's rule in that jurisdiction. For example, California, while adopting the Reasonableness test, has also adopted the fireman's rule and will apparently continue to apply it to police officers notwithstanding the acceptance of the reasonableness test. *See* Walters v. Sloan, 142 Cal. Rptr. 152, 571 P.2d 609 (1977).

58. Shypulski v. Waldorf Paper Prods. Co., 232 Minn. 394, 45 N.W.2d 549 (1951) (fireman).

59. *See, e.g.,* Hall v. Holton, 330 So.2d 81 (Fla. App. 1976) (owner knew police officers were making checks of premises).

60. *E.g.,* Murphy v. Ambassador E., 54 Ill. App. 3d 980, 370 N.E.2d 124 (1977) (officer caught hand in elevator door).

61. *See generally* 86 A.L.R.2d 1205, § 12 *et seq.* (1962). *See also* THE POLICE PLAINTIFF, 76-3, at 11.

POLICE RIGHTS

62. *See, e.g.,* Watson v. Kentucky & Ind. Bridge & R.R., 137 Ky. 619, 126 S.W. 146 (1910) (defendant negligently allowed gasoline spill, third party threw match into gasoline) (not a police case). *See generally* PROSSER, LAW OF TORTS § 44 (4th ed. 1971).

63. Ward v. State of New York, 81 Misc. 2d 583, 366 N.Y.S.2d 800 (Ct. Cl. 1975) (officers shot by armed guest at party at state hospital; court, expressing "sympathy" for "these two fine police officers," ruled act was unforeseeable by defendant premises owner).

64. Williams v. Wiewel, 36 Ill. App. 3d 478, 344 N.E.2d 34, 36-37 (1976) (quoting from the RESTATEMENT (SECOND) OF TORTS § 448). (Emphasis in opinion.) (Officer was shot by a person who had been asked by the premises owner to help defend the premises against burglars.)

65. Fancil v. Q.S.E. Foods, Inc., 60 Ill. 2d 552, 328 N.E.2d 538 (1975). The court in *Williams,* note 60 *supra,* distinguished the two cases on the grounds that in *Williams* the danger was not obvious to the officer. The *Fancil* case also suggests that getting shot from ambush by criminals is, to police officers, a "danger inherent in their occupation" — a view which could, if pursued by the courts, result in no recovery by any officer against anyone under any circumstances. *See* Assumption of Risk, Ch. 10 *infra.*

66. Walters v. Sloan, 142 Cal. Rptr. 152, 571 P.2d 609 (1977).

67. This is because at common law, existing rights of action in tort died with the plaintiff. Therefore, if the plaintiff expired before a judgment could be obtained, no recovery was possible. Every American jurisdiction now has a wrongful death statute to prevent this unfair result.

68. In some jurisdictions, the right of action is considered to belong to the deceased, in which case the amount recovered in the action will be added to the deceased's estate.

69. In some jurisdictions, because of the nature of the statute, the action may belong to the estate of the deceased, with any proceeds of the action going to that estate. The benefits will then pass eventually to the persons designated by will or the laws of intestate succession as beneficiaries of the estate.

70. *See* notes 68 and 69 *supra.*

71. Some of the cases cited in earlier sections of this chapter were wrongful death actions, *e.g.,* Fancil v. Q.S.E. Foods, Inc., note 61 *supra.* *See also* Smith v. County of Los Angeles, 276 Cal. App. 2d 156, 81 Cal. Rptr. 120 (1969) (judgment for heirs of officer killed in traffic accident while on duty: $373,839.77).

72. Klages v. General Ordinance Equip. Corp., 240 Pa. Sup. 356, 367 A.2d 304 (1976) (motel clerk used mace device against gunman, device failed to prevent gunman from shooting clerk; judgment for the plaintiff in the amount of $42,000 affirmed) (strict liability case).

124

73. If the equipment was not designed specifically for use in self-defense, failure of the equipment may not be recognized as a basis for a suit for injuries received from an attacker. *See* Williams v. RCA Corp., 59 Ill. App. 3d 229, 376 N.E.2d 37 (1978) (radio failure, call for help by security guard unheard by other units) (no recovery).

74. "The (defendant manufacturer) clearly recognized, or should have recognized, the possiblity of harm resulting to a purchaser if this weapon did not perform as represented. While the intervening criminal act of a third party can satisfy the requirements of a superseding cause, it does not do so where the criminal act is reasonably foreseeable." *Klages,* note 68 *supra,* at 313.

Chapter 6

ACTIONS FOR INFLICTION OF PSYCHOLOGICAL INJURIES

A. INFLICTION OF MENTAL DISTRESS

In the discussion in Chapter 3 of the elements of damages that are available in tort actions, it was pointed out that in personal injury actions, damages may be awarded not only for physical pain but also for mental anguish. Under earlier common-law tort principles, awards for mental suffering were limited to cases in which some other actionable injury had occurred; once other legally-recognized damage had been shown by the plaintiff, mental damage was compensable as well, but not otherwise. Thus, if the plaintiff could show, *e.g.,* negligent physical injury, or assault, battery, false imprisonment, etc., plaintiff could recover for mental suffering; otherwise not.[1]

Today, however, the opportunities for recovery for mental distress have vastly increased. Modern tort law provides a remedy where no physical or property injury has occurred, but the plaintiff has suffered injuries of a *purely mental or emotional nature.* This form of action, while not fully accepted in all jurisdictions, is now receiving wide approval as a form of redress for wrongs which would not have been compensable under earlier common-law principles.

There are two branches of this tort: *intentional* infliction of mental distress and *negligent* infliction of mental distress. Since the rules governing recovery differ markedly in the two categories, they will be discussed separately here.

1. *Intentional Infliction of Mental Distress*

a. General Considerations.

Where one person intentionally inflicts mental distress on another, the person suffering the distress has a right of action against the wrongdoer for money damages. The following points should be kept in mind:

(1) The conduct of the defendant must be flagrant and the mental distress suffered must be severe. The action does not lie for minor irritations or trivial insults. However, a prolonged series of minor actions by the defendant may be the basis for recovery.

Thus, for example, if the defendant has merely shouted "pig" at the police officer on one occasion, no action will be available for mental distress. As in defamation (see Chapter 8), "the law takes no notice of trifles." On the other hand, if the defendant has engaged in a protracted campaign of insults to the officer extending over a period of time, the cumulative effect of these numerous minor incidents may justify an action for mental distress.

Furthermore, one incident may be enough to support the action if that one incident is sufficiently flagrant.[2]

(2) There does not have to be any physical injury of any kind. Mental distress — by which is meant simply emotional upset — is sufficient basis for the action, and damages can be awarded for it.[3] This rule should be noted carefully. It applies only when the infliction of mental distress is intentional; the rule is otherwise if the defendant has merely been negligent (see below). Of course, if any physical injury does accompany the mental distress, it should be considered in awarding damages.

No actual contact of any kind with the body of the plaintiff is required. Mental distress may be intentionally inflicted by, *e.g.,* a long distance phone call.[4]

(3) The action will lie whenever the defendant acted for the specific purpose of causing emotional distress to the plaintiff officer, *and also where the defendant acted without such purpose but in a manner which was*

"substantially certain"[5] *to produce distress in the plaintiff.* For example, if the defendant were to beat up a member of the officer's family *for the purpose of causing distress to the officer,* the officer would have an action for intentional infliction of mental distress and the family member would, of course, have an action for battery. On the other hand, if the defendant beat up the family member because of some grudge against the family member and not for the purpose of causing mental distress to the officer, the officer would normally have no action for intentional infliction for mental distress, due to the lack of the intent element (although the family member would, of course, still have an action for battery). However, it has been held that where someone has been beaten up *in the presence of the plaintiff,* the plaintiff may maintain an action for intentional infliction of mental distress even though the assailants were not acting for the purpose of causing mental distress to the plaintiff. The rationale is that one witnessing a bloody beating, particularly if the victim is a loved one, is "substantially certain" to suffer mental distress. Therefore, *if the defendants knew that the plaintiff was present,* they are liable for intentional infliction of mental distress because they are regarded as having had knowledge to a substantial certainty that the plaintiff would suffer mental distress at the sight of the beating.[6]

b. Actions by Police Plaintiffs for Intentional Infliction of Mental Distress.

It appears that almost no use has been made by police plaintiffs of this tort action.[7] This may be due to several factors:

(a) Not all jurisdictions recognize it.

(b) Many potential plaintiffs are simply not aware that there is such an action.

(c) As noted earlier in the book, police officers have a marked reluctance to resort to litigation unless the case involves major physical injury or some form of attack on the officer's reputation.

Whatever the causes of this nonuse of this particular form of action, it appears that officer plaintiffs may be overlooking an excellent opportunity here. In the first place, the action is particularly suitable for the award of punitive damages; the maliciousness of the defendant's behavior is often sufficient to arouse the sympathy of the jury and move them to return a substantial figure in exemplary damages to punish the defendant for his (or her) vicious conduct. Secondly, it may be a very appropriate remedy where the officer's family has been victimized by a campaign of harassment against the officer. (See below.)

2. Negligent Infliction of Mental Distress

a. General Considerations.

Where the defendant's behavior is negligent rather than intentional, the possibilities of recovery are greatly reduced. The difference is traceable to the following rules applicable only to the negligent branch of the tort:

(1) Unlike intentional infliction of mental distress, where the distress is negligently inflicted most jurisdictions require a showing of *physical* injury before recovery can be allowed for the *emotional* harm done. No actual *impact* with the body of the plaintiff is required, however, and in this context, the term "physical injury" appears to mean merely that there must be some measurable physical *manifestation* associated with the mental upset.[8] A stress-induced heart attack or a miscarriage would certainly fulfill the requirement, but

far milder physical symptoms of stress have been held sufficient.

(2) In addition, in the tort of negligent infliction of mental distress, the courts usually limit recovery to situations where the mental distress results from some threat to the plaintiff himself, rather than to someone else. Thus, where the plaintiff has suffered distress as the result of observing a negligent injury to a third person, the plaintiff cannot usually recover unless the plaintiff was in the "zone of danger" — *i.e.,* was himself actually physically threatened by the negligent action of the defendant.[9]

Because this action does require a showing of negligence, all of the elements of negligence (duty, breach of duty, causation, and damages) must be shown, in addition to the special requirements listed above. The tort is not recognized in all jurisdictions, and there is considerable variation in the decisions even in states that have recognized the possibility of such a recovery.

b. Actions by Police Plaintiffs for Negligent Infliction of Mental Distress.

There has apparently been little use of this form of action by police plaintiffs. This does not mean that it is unavailable to police officers, however. For example, an officer directing traffic at an intersection narrowly missed by a drunken driver would, having been in the "zone of danger," presumably have a right of action for negligent infliction of mental distress if severe emotional trauma resulted from the near miss.

B. INSULTS, THREATS, AND HARASSMENT

1. *Insults*

Generally speaking, insults are not actionable. They are regarded by the law as trifles, for which no action is given in the ordinary case either in mental distress, defamation, or any other form of common-law action.

Statutes may come into play here, however. For example, Prosser notes that three states, Virginia, Mississippi, and West Virginia, have statutes which make ordinary insults civilly actionable.[10] These statutes grow out of the old anti-dueling codes, and are intended to discourage any conduct tending toward a breach of the peace. For example, Virginia's statute reads: "All words shall be actionable which from their usual construction and common acceptance are construed as insults and tend to violence and breach." [11] Insults may also become actionable if they are repeated to the point that it becomes a continued course of conduct inflicting severe emotional distress upon the plaintiff, in which case the action is simply one for intentional infliction of mental distress. (See above.)

2. *Threats*

At common law, a verbal threat, unaccompanied by any gesture sufficient to constitute assault, was not civilly actionable, a situation which caused Dean Prosser to observe that ". . . the result was a rule which permitted recovery for a gesture that might frighten the plaintiff for a moment, and denied it for menacing words which kept him in terror of his life for a month." [12]

Today threats may be civilly actionable by statute, or, when uttered repeatedly, they may constitute a flagrant course of conduct actionable for intentional infliction of mental distress.

3. *Harassment*

As noted above, harassment generally falls within the area of intentional infliction of mental distress if it is actionable at all.[13] Harassment of family members may be actionable. (See below.)

C. ACTIONS BY THE FAMILY OF THE OFFICER

Campaigns of harassment against police officers often directly affect members of the officer's family. When this is the case, the family members so affected have causes of action in their own right. This has been discussed in Chapter 3, but additional emphasis is appropriate here. Thus, the family member affected may have a right of action under statute, or for intentional infliction of mental distress or other common-law torts in many situations, including the following:

1. Obscene or threatening phone calls; telephone answered by officer's spouse, child, parent, etc.

2. False message — by telephone, telegraph, or any other means — that the officer has been injured or killed; message communicated to family member.

3. Family pet injured or killed for the purpose of causing distress to the officer.

4. Injury to the officer in the family member's presence.

5. Direct injury to the family member, including beating, kidnapping, etc.

6. Injury to jointly-owned property — home, etc.

These are only examples; the fact is that *any* act which causes direct injury to the officer's family is actionable by the family members affected, and may, of course, give the officer a cause of action as well for mental distress, loss of consortium, etc.

D. ASSAULT

It is sometimes said that one reason for allowing an action for assault, where there is no physical injury or even physical contact, is to compensate the plaintiff for the fright or other mental discomfort suffered. In a sense, then, the tort of assault might well be regarded as a right of action for psychological injury and could therefore be included in this chapter. Because of its close association with the tort of battery, however, it has been included in the chapter on personal injuries (Chapter 5 *supra*), despite the fact that no actual physical injury is usually involved.

CHAPTER 6 — NOTES

1. The award of damages for mental distress was thus formerly "parasitic" in nature; availability of compensation depended upon the existence of some other recognized form of injury. *See* PROSSER, LAW OF TORTS § 12, at 52 (4th ed. 1971).

2. *E.g.,* bringing a lynch mob to plaintiff's door. PROSSER, LAW OF TORTS § 12, at 56 (4th ed. 1971).

3. *See generally* PROSSER, LAW OF TORTS § 12 (4th ed. 1971).

4. In fact, a classic example of behavior which has been held actionable is the telephone call which intentionally falsely informs the person called that a loved one has been killed or injured. *See* Injuries to the Officer's Family *infra.*

5. *See* the discussion of Intent in Ch. 5 *supra.*

6. *See, e.g.,* Taylor v. Vallelunga, 171 Cal. App. 2d 107, 339 P.2d 910 (1959) (father beaten up in daughter's presence) (not a police case).

7. In one case, McCart v. Morris, 58 App. Div. 2d 700, 396 N.Y.S.2d 107 (1977), three state policemen sued for libel, slander, and intentional infliction of mental distress. The complaint was dismissed on other grounds without discussion of the mental distress issue. *The Police Plaintiff* also reported one trial court case, Dean v. Valliere, Superior Ct., Tulare County, Cal. (1976) (THE POLICE PLAINTIFF 77-1, at 7).

8. This requirement has been adopted by the courts in the hope of reducing the number of fraudulent claims.

9. *See generally* PROSSER, LAW OF TORTS § 54 (4th ed. 1971).

10. PROSSER, LAW OF TORTS § 12, at 55 (4th ed. 1971).

11. VA. CODE § 18.01-45. The action is closely related to defamation and the statute has often been interpreted by the same rules applicable to libel and slander. Insults tending toward a breach of the peace may also be punishable as crimes. *See, e.g.,* VA. CODE § 18.2-417. (Class 3 misdemeanor.)

12. PROSSER, LAW OF TORTS 52 (4th ed. 1971). Threats, like insults, may also be punishable criminally, of course.

13. *Cf.* Jeffers v. Seattle, Superior Ct., King County, Wash. (1977), reported in *The Police Plaintiff* as an action for "harassment." THE POLICE PLAINTIFF, 78-1, at 8.

Chapter 7

ACTIONS FOR IMPROPERLY SUBJECTING THE OFFICER TO LEGAL PROCESS OR PHYSICAL CONFINEMENT

The actions of malicious prosecution, abuse of process, false arrest, and false imprisonment have certain technical characteristics in common. In addition, more than one of these actions may arise from the same incident. Indeed, it would not be difficult to hypothesize a factual situation in which one defendant simultaneously or successively commits *all four torts.* In addition, factual situations involving these four torts often involve assault, battery, and/or defamation as well.[1]

Consequently, while these actions are discussed separately in this book, potential plaintiffs should keep in mind that one incident may give rise to several separate torts, all actionable, with damages awardable for each of the several torts committed by the defendant.

A. MALICIOUS PROSECUTION

1. *General Considerations*

a. False Criminal Charges.

Where a person has made false charges of criminal behavior against an officer, these charges are of course usually actionable as libel or slander. In addition, however, where the person making the charges has set in motion a criminal prosecution against the officer involved, the officer may also have a right to sue for the tort of "malicious prosecution." Malicious prosecution is one of the most complicated and difficult to maintain of all tort actions, and each of the numerous elements of the tort must be proven before a recovery can be obtained. To obtain a judgment, the officer must prove (1) that the defendant initiated a criminal action against the officer; (2) that this was done without probable cause;[2] (3) that the criminal action was eventually terminated in a manner favorable to the officer; (4) that the defendant acted with malice (which in this case means "spite" or "ill will"); and (5) that the officer suffered damages.[3]

The courts have not favored malicious prosecution actions because of the possible deterrent effect of such suits upon persons who believe in good faith that a crime has been committed but might fail to report it for fear of civil liability. Nevertheless, where the officer has been subjected to criminal prosecution by virtue of a false charge, a malicious prosecution action should be considered, since this remedy may be available in situations where a recovery in libel or slander is not possible.

b. Malicious Prosecution Actions Based upon Prior Civil Actions.

Some states permit malicious prosecution actions to be brought by persons who have been subjected to unfounded civil actions. The prerequisites for recovery are basically the same as for prior criminal actions, and include the requirement of "no probable cause." Since in the case of prior civil actions "probable cause" seems to mean nothing more than that the action is brought in good faith and is not obviously without legal basis, it is even harder to obtain a recovery in malicious prosecution for a prior civil suit than it is to recover for a prior criminal charge, and successful recoveries are few even in the states which permit them in theory.

c. Malicious Prosecution Actions Based upon Administrative Proceedings.

Many jurisdictions now permit malicious prosecution actions for false charges leading to hearings before an administrative body, at least where the administrative tribunal has disciplinary or punitive powers.[4]

2. Suits by Police Plaintiffs for Malicious Prosecution

a. Generally.

Compared to other torts such as battery and defamation, there have been relatively few suits by officers for malicious prosecution. This is probably traceable in part to the extreme difficulty any plaintiff encounters in obtaining a recovery for malicious prosecution; the numerous, highly technical elements of the tort; and the general attitude of disfavor with which the tort has been regarded by the courts discourage all plaintiffs, of whatever profession, from even attempting the action.

Police plaintiffs face an additional obstacle; suits by police officers for malicious prosecution against citizens who have previously made charges against the officer are often severely criticized on the grounds that the bringing of such suits by police against complaining citizens tends to intimidate citizens with legitimate complaints against the police and to prevent such citizens from exercising their rights.[5]

Nevertheless, the increasing number of false complaints and charges being made against police officers may be causing the courts to be more receptive to actions for malicious prosecution by the officers involved. In addition, police associations and others are starting to encourage malicious prosecution actions as a matter of policy, to try to stem the flood of malicious and unfounded charges being made against officers in most urban areas today.[6] One authority urges that municipalities and departments also encourage malicious prosecution actions; such encouragement will, it is felt, "... increase morale among the officers; and it will give the department a stern 'no-nonsense' image." [7]

139

A number of cases have in fact been brought by officers for malicious prosecution, most of them growing out of false complaints filed after an arrest by the person arrested. These unfounded charges often take the form of an immediate lawsuit or criminal warrant against the officer, or there may be simply complaints filed with internal affairs divisions (IAD). In the latter situation, it should be noted that it has been held that the fact that a complaint to IAD or some other departmental body results in an internal investigation of the officer is not sufficient to justify a recovery for malicious prosecution. A California court has observed that

> ... a mere investigation which does not lead to the initiation of proceedings before an administrative board having power to take action adversely affecting plaintiff's legally protected interests is not a sufficient basis upon which to found a malicious prosecution action....[8]

The plaintiff officer will therefore be able to maintain an action for malicious prosecution only where some formal legal proceeding, as distinguished from a mere investigation, has been wrongfully initiated against the officer by the defendant.[9]

Where officers have been successful in obtaining a recovery for malicious prosecution, the damages awarded may vary widely because of the fact that specific pecuniary damages do not normally have to be proven. One officer collected $101;[10] another has filed an action for malicious prosecution and other torts asking damages totalling $7.5 million dollars.[11]

b. Actions Against Attorneys.

It appears that malicious prosecution may be a suitable method of gaining redress against attorneys engaged in unfounded litigation against police officers. Every major urban area seems to include one or more attorneys who habitually engage in litigation against police officers or departments, often when no justification for such litigation exists either in law or in fact. Recent developments in the law indicate that these members of the legal profession may no longer be immune from legal process themselves.

The landmark cases here have involved physicians; in several cases, doctors have recovered judgments from the *lawyers* of former patients who filed baseless malpractice actions against the doctors.[12] Other cases involving plaintiffs of different types have recognized the principle that attorneys may be held liable for malicious prosecution for bringing an action which the attorney does not reasonably believe to be justified.[13]

Officers who have been subjected to some form of legal harassment by unethical attorneys may wish to consider filing a malicious prosecution action against the attorney; such actions have the dual attraction of providing a deep pocket from which a judgment may be satisfied and discouraging the attorney from filing similar actions against fellow officers in the future.[14]

In summary it may be said that the malicious prosecution action is available, and that, although difficult, recovery is possible and the damage award may be substantial.[15]

B. ABUSE OF PROCESS

1. *General Considerations*

Because of the similarity between abuse of process and malicious prosecution, these two torts are often confused. They both involve the misuse of the machinery of justice, and certain factual situations might fall into either or both categories.

Basically, the difference is that in malicious prosecution, the process of the court (*e.g.,* the arrest warrant) has been *obtained* wrongfully under circumstances in which it should never have been issued at all (because of no probable cause, etc.). On the other hand, a suit for abuse of process will lie where the process was rightfully obtained *but is thereafter used for a wrongful purpose,* thereby perverting it. If, for example, someone *did* have probable cause to obtain a warrant of arrest against an officer, and did so, but then used that warrant as a means of extorting money or favors from the officer, the proper action would be abuse of process, not malicious prosecution.[16]

Abuse of process is less technical than malicious prosecution and therefore easier to maintain when appropriate to the facts. For example, no "favorable termination" of the proceedings need be shown; the action may be brought even while the other proceeding against the officer is still going on. The only requirement is that the proceeding or process, though lawful in its inception, is now being *misused* in some manner.[17]

2. *Abuse of Process Suits by Police Plaintiffs*

Abuse of process is a tort remedy which is seldom used by anyone, and still less often used by police plaintiffs. A survey of all cases in the author's files and all cases reported in *The Police Plaintiff* over the past two years revealed no police plaintiff cases identifiable as true abuse of process cases.[18] While this does not, of course, mean that no such suits have been filed, it does indicate that, proportionately at least, true abuse of process suits by police plaintiffs are rare. Nevertheless, as suggested above, the action might lie in any situation in which any person, having just cause to do so, has instituted legal proceedings or obtained a legal process against the officer and is now trying to use the threat of further proceedings to intimidate the officer or to extort money or favors from the officer.[19]

C. FALSE IMPRISONMENT

1. *General Considerations*

When one person intentionally confines another without a legal right to do so, the person confined may have an action for false imprisonment. The action is not as complex as malicious prosecution, but the following requirements must be noted:

a. There Must Be a "Confinement."

However, this need not be a confinement in the sense that someone has been locked up in a cell, although that would certainly be included. In fact, false imprisonment may lie where the plaintiff was physically confined in *any* manner (as by being locked in an ordinary room or vehicle, or tied up or handcuffed), or has been confined verbally, as by an order not to move or not to leave a certain area under threat of legal action or other penalty.[20] However, merely blocking one route of travel where others are available is not normally "confinement" for this purpose.

b. The Confinement Must Be Intentional.

If the defendant has, for example, inadvertently locked up a room not knowing that someone was inside, there can be no false imprisonment action. The intent required here is the *intent to confine;* even negligence is not enough.

c. The Confinement Must Be Wrongful.

The word "false" in the term "false imprisonment" means simply that the confinement, to be actionable, must be *wrongful.* If there is legal justification for the confinement, there can be no false imprisonment action for it.

Note, however, that a mistake as to one's *right* to confine the plaintiff is not a defense, even though the mistake is made in good faith. Thus, for example, if someone locks up

143

an undercover police officer in the mistaken belief that the officer is a criminal, the fact that the mistake was made reasonably and in good faith is no defense to the action, although good faith will prevent an award of punitive damages. No actual damages need be shown to maintain this action.

2. *Suits for False Imprisonment by Police Plaintiffs*

The action of false imprisonment appears to be seldom used by officer plaintiffs. Possibly this is because in most such incidents involving officers the actual damage to the officer is either very minor, and is therefore ignored, or very great, in which case actions for battery or wrongful death may be more appropriate. Officers should note, however, that the remedy is available in situations where there is no physical injury or other actual damage; and even though situations in which a police officer has been the victim of false imprisonment usually include assault and battery as well, the officer is entitled to sue for *all* of these torts and recover damages for *each*.

Line-of-duty situations which might give rise to an action for false imprisonment might include:

1. Being held at gunpoint, *e.g.,* as a hostage. (The type of weapon is usually not material; the same tort would be involved if a knife, explosives, etc. were used.)

2. Being tied up or handcuffed (even if the handcuffs belong to the officer).

3. Being prevented by a mob from leaving the officer's present location.

4. Being locked in any room, vehicle, or container (*e.g.,* a bank vault).

These are illustrative only; any restriction of the officer's movements, whether due to physical restraint or threats, may be false imprisonment.[21] Again, note that the act which gives rise to the false imprisonment action may include other torts as well, such as assault, battery, mental distress, etc., all of which are actionable. The officer does not have to choose between them, but may assert *all* causes of action arising out of an incident. Battery is an especially frequent companion of false imprisonment.

Again, note that no physical injury need be shown, and that punitive damages may be available.[22]

D. FALSE ARREST

1. *General Considerations*

When a person is arrested without lawful authority, the arrestee has a right of action for "false arrest." In reality, false arrest is a form of false imprisonment, the "confinement" being the legal constraint imposed by being placed in the status of being under arrest. This legal constraint exists regardless of physical constraint or the lack of it, and may occur, *e.g.,* when a person is unlawfully arrested in the middle of an open field without a hand being laid upon the arrestee. Note that:

a. *In false arrest actions, or in criminal law, an "arrest" may occur without the utterance of the phrase "you are under arrest."* Any attempt to restrict the movements of the plaintiff by *improper assertion of legal authority* may be an "arrest" if the plaintiff understands that he is being restricted in that manner by the defendant.

b. The fact that the wrong person has been arrested does not make the arrest unlawful or "false." A reasonable or good faith mistake *may* protect the defendant from liability, depending upon the law of the particular jurisdiction. Only arrests that are unlawful in the sense of being in excess of the power of arrest as granted to the defendant in that jurisdiction are "false."

c. *Civilian citizens as well as police officers may be liable for false arrest.* (In fact, a civilian may be more

145

likely to be guilty of making an unlawful arrest than an officer, because the ordinary citizen's right of arrest is so limited that many so-called "citizen's arrests" are actually unlawful.)

2. *Suits by Police Plaintiffs for False Arrest*

Relatively few actions by police plaintiffs for false arrest have been found. Interestingly enough, in a majority of the cases which have been found the defendant was the employer or superior of the plaintiff officer, and the cases arose as the result of some charge being placed against the officer by his superiors.[23] It appears that in at least some of these instances, what is being termed "false arrest" may actually be malicious prosecution.

However, if the officer is in fact arrested unlawfully, as where a misdemeanor arrest is made without a warrant under circumstances not justifying a warrantless arrest, or a warrantless felony arrest is made without probable cause, a true false arrest suit may lie against the fellow officers making the arrest.[24]

The lack of false arrest cases involving unlawful arrests of officers by citizens probably reflects the infrequency of such incidents; the momentary nature of the "arrest"; the good faith of the citizen; and the lack of serious injury to the officer. In most cases, the officer would probably just like to forget the whole thing. When the arrest is made by a supervisor or other sworn personnel, however, it is usually part of an extended proceeding which has serious disciplinary or other professional consequences for the officer; hence the greater likelihood of a false arrest action.

As with false imprisonment, the situation giving rise to the action for false arrest may also include other torts, such as battery or defamation, for which damages may also be obtained.[25]

146

CHAPTER 7 — NOTES

1. *See, e.g.,* THE POLICE PLAINTIFF, 78-1, at 3, discussing a case in which the plaintiff officer reportedly sued for (1) assault, (2) battery, (3) false imprisonment, (4) malicious prosecution, and (5) defamation.

2. Probable cause is used here in the same sense that it is used in criminal law. It should be noted, however, that if the charge is *true,* and the officer is actually guilty, that is conclusive evidence that there *was* probable cause. In effect, then, only *false* charges are actionable in malicious prosecution.

3. Although for historical reasons it has been customary to say that there can be no recovery in malicious prosecution without actual damages, in most jurisdictions damages are assumed or are awarded without the necessity of specific proof. *See* PROSSER, LAW OF TORTS 849 (4th ed. 1971).

4. *E.g.,* California. *See* Hardy v. Vial, 48 Cal. 2d 577, 311 P.2d 494 (1957), approving the rule of the RESTATEMENT (SECOND) OF TORTS § 680 permitting such actions.

5. *See* Ch. 10 *infra.*

6. *See* Ch. 1 *supra.*

7. *Countersuits for Malicious Prosecution,* THE POLICE PLAINTIFF, 77-1, at 10, 13.

8. Imig v. Ferrar, 70 Cal. App. 3d 48, 138 Cal. Rptr. 540, 545 (1977).

9. Notice, however, that an *initiation* of legal proceedings is normally sufficient; *it is generally not necessary that an actual hearing or trial be held.* For example, if the defendant causes an indictment to be obtained, or a preliminary hearing to be held, or even obtains a warrant against the officer, that is usually held to be adequate foundation for a malicious prosecution action.

10. THE POLICE PLAINTIFF, 76-3, at 9.

11. THE POLICE PLAINTIFF, 78-1, at 3.

12. *See* Ch. 3, note 69 *supra.*

13. *E.g.,* Norton v. Hines, 49 Cal. App. 3d 917, 123 Cal. Rptr. 237 (1975) (plaintiff could recover against opponent's attorney for malicious prosecution but not for negligence) (not a police case). But actual damages must be shown. Pantone v. Demos, 59 Ill. App. 3d 328, 375 N.E.2d 480 (1978) (not a police case).

14. For further discussion of such suits, *see* THE POLICE PLAINTIFF, 77-1, at 10-13. The article points out that, in addition to suit, such attorneys are subject to disciplinary action by the bar and the courts.

15. As to malicious prosecution generally, *see* PROSSER, LAW OF TORTS § 119 (4th ed. 1971); and 52 AM. JUR. 2d *Malicious Prosecution* (1970).

16. Some jurisdictions may limit abuse of process to civil process. *See, e.g.,* Hatcher v. Moree, 133 Ga. App. 14, 209 S.E.2d 708 (1974) (not a police case).

17. *See generally* PROSSER, LAW OF TORTS § 121 (4th ed. 1971).

18. THE POLICE PLAINTIFF, 76-3, at 7, reports a "misuse of process" case; this term, often used to cover both malicious prosecution and abuse of process, appears in this case to refer to a malicious prosecution situation.

19. As to abuse of process generally, *see* PROSSER, LAW OF TORTS § 121 (4th ed. 1971); 1 AM. JUR. 2d *Abuse of Process* (1962).

20. False arrest, discussed below, is actually a form of false imprisonment. *See* below.

21. Where the officer is required by regulation to take a breath test when suspected of drinking on duty, the citizen making the allegation is not liable for false imprisonment. Dellinger v. Belk, 34 N.C. App. 488, 238 S.E.2d 788 (1977).

22. *See generally* PROSSER, LAW OF TORTS § 11 (4th ed. 1971); and 32 AM. JUR. 2d *False Imprisonment* (1967).

23. *See, e.g.,* THE POLICE PLAINTIFF, 77-4, at 6 (defendants: city, police chief, police captain; judgment for plaintiff officer, $50,000) and THE POLICE PLAINTIFF, 77-1, at 8 (false arrest and defamation suit against defendant police chief; judgment for plaintiff officer, $500).

24. *See, e.g.,* THE POLICE PLAINTIFF, 76-1, at 6 (warrantless felony arrest by officers on citizen complaint; plaintiff alleged lack of probable cause for arrest and sued, among others, the two officers who arrested him).

25. As to false arrest generally, *see* PROSSER, LAW OF TORTS 45-46 (4th ed. 1971); 32 AM. JUR. 2d *False Imprisonment* (1967); and 5 AM. JUR. 2d *Arrest* (1962).

Chapter 8

ACTIONS FOR INJURIES TO THE PLAINTIFF'S REPUTATION OR PROFESSIONAL STATUS

A. DEFAMATION

1. *General Considerations*

When one utters false and derogatory statements about another person, the person about whom the statements are made may have an action for defamation. Defamation actually consists of two separate torts — libel and slander. Where the defamatory matter is spoken orally, both the wrong and the remedy are called "slander"; where the derogatory words are preserved in permanent form, as in writing or print or on film or tape, the tort is "libel." [1]

Although the two torts have different historical backgrounds and are theoretically separate and distinct, they have certain aspects in common, as discussed below.

a. The Statement Must Be Defamatory.

Not every derogatory statement is actionable. The statement must be of such a nature that significant injury will be done to the reputation of the plaintiff. Various legal formulas have been suggested to establish what is defamatory; thus, for example, many courts have said that the plaintiff must show that the defendant's statements caused the plaintiff to be "held up to hatred, contempt, or ridicule, or to be shunned or avoided." [2] Thus, the fact that a statement may be derogatory or insulting is not alone sufficient; casual insults or epithets, for example, are normally not actionable in defamation, because they are not regarded as being sufficiently harmful to warrant invocation of the law's processes. Although some courts have held that only statements of fact are actionable, it appears that merely labeling the statement as a "rumor," or even as an "opinion,"

149

will not relieve the defendant of liability if specific accusations are included. Nevertheless, expressions of opinion which do not purport to have any specific or factual basis *may* not be actionable. (See also the discussion of the "fair comment" privilege, below.)

b. The Statement Must Identify the Plaintiff.

The plaintiff does not have a cause of action in libel or slander unless the defendant's statement identified the plaintiff as being the subject of the statement. This does not mean that the plaintiff must be named specifically, but the content or context of the statement must be such that persons reading or hearing the statement will understand that the plaintiff is being referred to. For this reason, members of very large groups will not be able to sue for statements about the group as a whole.

c. The Statement Must Be False.

To be actionable, the statement must be *false.* There is no right of action for a statement which is true. This creates problems when the statement is partly true or is a mere expression of opinion. Generally speaking, if the statement is *substantially* true, the defendant is not liable.

d. There Must Be "Publication."

In order for the statement to be actionable, it must have been communicated in some manner to third persons. This communication is called "publication" regardless of the form of communication. Thus, a derogatory statement made by the defendant solely to the plaintiff is not actionable unless someone else reads or overhears it.

e. Damage Must Be Shown.

In order for the plaintiff to recover for defamation, damages must be shown. Slander normally requires proof of "special" — *i.e.,* pecuniary — damage. Certain types of slander, however, require only a showing of "general" damage, which today appears to mean actual damage of a nonpecuniary type, such as humiliation, etc.[3] Slander which accuses the plaintiff of (1) a serious crime, (2) a "loathesome disease" (*i.e.,* leprosy or V.D.), (3) unfitness for his or her trade or profession, (4) unchastity, if plaintiff is a female, or (5) (in some jurisdictions) homosexuality is called "slander *per se*" and requires no showing of special damages. Libel, whatever the accusation, normally requires no showing of special (pecuniary) damages,[4] but actual damage of some sort will now apparently have to be shown.[5]

The determination of whether the defamatory statement is slander, slander *per se*, or libel is extremely important because of this difference in the required proof of damages. It is usually very difficult for the plaintiff to show special (pecuniary) damages; consequently, it is much easier to recover for libel or slander *per se* than for other types of slander.

f. The Defendant Must Have Been at "Fault."

Formerly, one could be held liable for defamation despite lack of fault — actually a form of strict liability. Today, however, it appears that the defendant is not liable *in any case* unless the defendant was in some way at fault, *i.e.,* defamed the plaintiff intentionally or through negligence.[6]

g. Defenses.

Libel and slander actions can be defeated by any one of several defenses; one of these, truth, has already been mentioned. Perhaps the most significant defense in the present context is the defense of "privilege."

(1) *"Privilege" Generally.*

Under certain circumstances, the defendant may be "privileged" to make statements about the plaintiff which

151

are both derogatory and false. If there is a "privilege," the plaintiff cannot recover.

Privileges are of two major types: *absolute* and *qualified.* If the defendant has an *absolute* privilege, it means that he or she is not liable for defamatory statements about the plaintiff *even if defendant knew the statements were false.* If the defendant has a *qualified* privilege, defendant is protected *only if defendant believed the words were true.*

Absolute privilege is granted to all persons engaged in certain occupations or duties at the time that the derogatory statements are made. For example, judges, lawyers, witnesses, and jurors enjoy an *absolute* privilege for statements made within the scope of judicial proceedings. Similarly, legislators and high governmental officials are absolutely privileged while acting in their official capacities.[7]

By contrast, a *qualified* privilege may exist in *any* person in *any* situation in which the defendant acts in good faith to protect legitimate interests of his own or of others.

A qualified privilege of "fair comment" about the conduct of public officials was well established in the law prior to the *New York Times* case, described below. This "fair comment" privilege was, in a majority of states, limited to opinion and critical comment, and would not protect a defendant who made misstatements of *fact.* Nevertheless, it was felt that the public interest was served by permitting open discussion of the performance of those in public office, and such comment was privileged as long as it was made in good faith and without malice.

(2) *Constitutional Privilege: The Rule in New York Times v. Sullivan.*

In the case of *New York Times v. Sullivan,*[8] the Supreme Court of the United States ruled that plaintiffs who are "public officials" cannot recover for libel or slander unless they can establish that the defendant acted with *knowledge that the statement was false or with "reckless disregard" of the statement's truth or falsity.* (The Court somewhat confusingly referred to this element — knowledge of falsity or reckless disregard of truth or falsity — as "malice," although this usage is different from the common-law meaning of that term.) This requirement was subsequently extended to cover "public figures," a term which includes private citizens as well as those in public office.[9]

Many thousands of words have been written about *New York Times v. Sullivan* and the many cases which have interpreted and expanded its holding.[10] The net result of the case and its progeny was the creation of a constitutional privilege, based on the First Amendment, to publish false derogatory statements about "public officials" and "public figures." Because this defense can be overcome only by showing that the defendant *knew* the statement was false or acted with *reckless disregard* of truth or falsity, the chances of success in a defamation action brought by any plaintiff falling into the "public official" or "public figure" category have been sharply reduced, since such proof is very difficult to obtain.

This rule has had an extremely serious impact on police officers attempting to recover for defamation. (See below.)

(3) *Bad Reputation, Retraction, Malice.*

The fact that the plaintiff already has a bad reputation is not a complete defense. It does, however, bear on the question of damages. Similarly, in the absence of statute, printing a retraction does not bar the action, but may mitigate damages and may be relevant on the question of actual malice.

If the defendant is not a public official or public figure, no showing of actual malice is normally required. Negligence is enough. However, actual malice may be relevant on questions of qualified privilege and punitive damages. Lack of actual malice may therefore be an absolute defense where qualified privilege exists, but is otherwise not a bar to the recovery of compensatory damages.[11]

2. *Defamation Actions by Police Plaintiffs*

a. Police Plaintiff Cases Generally.

Defamation of police officers is not exactly a new problem; the earliest case cited in this section occurred in 1886. Nevertheless, utterance or publication of defamatory statements about law enforcement personnel is becoming increasingly common; these verbal attacks have apparently increased in frequency in recent years at an astounding rate.

The causes of the trend are complex, but it seems probable that the increasingly anti-police attitude manifested in our society over the past few years, and the adoption of verbal attacks on police as a tactical and strategic policy by various organized groups, are at least in part responsible.

Because of the increasing number of such attacks, and for the other reasons suggested in Chapter 1, police officers, urged on by many police associations, have been increasingly resorting to the civil courts to obtain redress and to attempt to discourage similar attacks in the future.[12] For reasons that will be pointed out later in this chapter, recovery for libel or slander can be difficult for a law enforcement officer, but the suits are being brought and some, at least, are successful.

b. Police Plaintiffs.

Defamatory attacks on the police have not been restricted to any one level of authority. As a result, plaintiffs range from ordinary patrolmen [13] to police chiefs,[14] deputy superintendents,[15] and police commissioners.[16] The list includes deputy sheriffs,[17] sheriffs,[18] deputy marshals,[19]

154

marshals,[20] lieutenants,[21] captains,[22] deputy chiefs,[23] state police officers,[24] federal agents,[25] former officers,[26] and even candidates for elective law enforcement positions.[27]

Often, of course, the defamatory remarks are directed at more than one officer, or at entire departments. In the former case, the individual officers, if named or otherwise specifically identified, may all bring suit, but defamation of an entire department, or of unidentified individuals within the department, may not be actionable because the group is too large.[28] For this reason, class actions may fail, at least where the class is large.[29]

c. Defendants in Police Plaintiff Cases.

Newspapers and their owners, publishers, and editors appear to be the most frequent defendants,[30] but in many instances the defamatory statements have emanated from persons whom the plaintiff officer has arrested[31] or ticketed.[32] City and county officials, including the plaintiff's own supervisors and other officers are often named as defendants.[33] Candidates for public office are sometimes defendants,[34] as are civil rights groups,[35] legislators,[36] magazine publishers,[37] owners of broadcasting stations,[38] clergymen,[39] attorneys,[40] judges,[41] and even civic groups.[42]

The foregoing list is, of course, merely illustrative; potentially almost anyone may be named as a defendant. In many instances, however, persons in particular occupations or positions will enjoy immunity or privilege which protects them from suit.[43]

d. Defamatory Statements in Police Plaintiff Cases.

(1) *Definitions of Defamation in Police Plaintiff Cases.*

In police plaintiff cases the courts have followed the generally accepted definitions of defamation, including the "hatred, contempt or ridicule" formula discussed above, and

155

its many variations.[44] Defendant may be liable for what is insinuated as well as for what is stated explicitly.[45]

(2) *Statements Actionable in Police Plaintiff Cases.*

There seems to be no question that charges of brutality, corruption, harassment, immorality, lying, unjustified arrest, unfitness, unbecoming conduct, shakedowns, fabrication of evidence, improper use of firearms, theft, burglary, murder, or any other serious crime are all actionable.[46] In the proper context, even much milder accusations have been found defamatory, as in one case in which a recovery was obtained for statements that the officer had "limited training," "no culture," and was a "professional moocher." [47] Ridicule may be actionable even if no specific charge is made, as in the case in which the defendant newspaper editor printed an article suggesting that the town marshal be put in a cage and placed on public display.[48]

(3) *Methods of Publication in Police Plaintiff Cases.*

Methods of dissemination of defamation have included not only media publications and false complaints to police departments, but also news conferences,[49] mailing out letters to area residents,[50] and passing out handbills.[51]

(4) *Nonverbal Defamation in Police Plaintiff Cases.*

Words are not necessary; an action may be maintained where the officer is unfavorably depicted in a cartoon or caricature.[52] Juxtaposition of a photograph of the defendant with words suggesting misconduct may be actionable.[53]

(5) *Identification of Plaintiff in Police Plaintiff Cases.*

The statement must identify the plaintiff officer in some manner. Statements alleging that some unidentified members of a department are guilty of misconduct have been held insufficient where a large department is involved.[54]

(6) *Opinion in Police Plaintiff Cases.*

In one case, a trial court reportedly dismissed an action on the grounds that the statements were restricted to "opinions and judgments." [55] As noted above, this does not necessarily protect the defendant, and the result might be otherwise in a different court.

e. Damages in Police Plaintiff Cases.

In the defamation cases in the author's files in which the plaintiff officer was awarded a known amount in damages, jury verdicts ranged from $750 to $250,000. The $250,000 judgment was an unusually large one; if it is disregarded, the average recovery per officer for all other cases tried was only $7,273.91. In addition, a number of cases were settled without trial; the range was from $5 to $25,000. Again, the latter settlement was disproportionately large by comparison with most of the settlements, which, without inclusion of the $25,000 case, averaged only $800.62 per officer.

It appears that many of the cases were brought as a matter of principle rather than with any real expectation of collecting a large amount of money. As one officer who settled for $5 reportedly put it, "the money was not the purpose of the suit. The whole purpose of the suit was personal vindication." [56]

If the officer's reputation was bad even before the defendant's statements, evidence of that bad reputation is admissible to mitigate damages. [57]

f. Defenses in Police Plaintiff Cases.

(1) *Truth.*

Truth is a defense in police plaintiff cases as in any defamation action, and here also it is sufficient if the statement is *substantially* true, if the defendant had a good motive and was acting toward a just end. [58] But it has been

157

held that a statement attributing misconduct to a police official is not "true" merely because *subordinates* were guilty of misconduct, unless the plaintiff official actually *knew* of the misconduct.[59]

(2) *Sovereign Immunity.*

Where the defendant is a municipal corporation or other governmental body, the problem of sovereign immunity may arise. (See Chapter 10.) However, it has been held that where city officials engaged in a conspiracy to defame the plaintiff officer and have him discharged, sovereign immunity would not protect the city from liability.[60]

(3) *Common-Law Privileges.*

(a) Qualified Privilege — General. Defendant may be privileged to discuss the officer with persons who have a legitimate interest in the officer's affairs. Thus, for example, statements made by police supervisors in response to an inquiry from the plaintiff officer's relatives have been held to be qualifiedly privileged.[61]

(b) Qualified Privilege — Fair Comment. Prior to the decision in *New York Times v. Sullivan,* several courts had expressly recognized the existence of the privilege of "fair comment," discussed above, in cases involving police plaintiffs.[62] This privilege was defeated however, if there was "malice" in the sense of intent to injure, and malice could be presumed from the nature of the statements.[63] Even after the *New York Times* case, this qualified privilege continues to exist in theory, and it has been expressly recognized in cases decided since *New York Times.*[64] However, it appears that it has been virtually swallowed up by the *New York Times* rule, which extends far beyond the common-law privilege.

The existence of any such privilege is determined by the judge, not by the jury.[65]

(c) Absolute Privilege for Statements Made in the Course of Official Proceedings. It has been held that statements made by police officials in connection with departmental hearings are absolutely privileged.[66] Some courts have held that statements made by complaining citizens in connection with departmental investigations of the officer plaintiff are also absolutely privileged — a view which, if widely adopted, would virtually put an end to suits for false complaints, since one who has an absolute privilege is not liable even though he *knew* the statement was false.[67]

Even where an absolute privilege exists, however, it applies only when the statement is made in the course of and relevant to the official proceedings; statements made to the press or in other contexts not directly connected with the proceeding should not be privileged. The absolute privilege of judges and attorneys, for example, may be defeated by showing that the statements were made outside of the courtroom or otherwise were not within the scope of the judicial proceedings.[68]

(d) Constitutional Privilege to Defame Public Officials: *New York Times v. Sullivan*'s Effect upon Police Plaintiffs. As noted earlier, the case of *New York Times v. Sullivan*[69] established the rule that a public official may not recover for defamation unless the defendant acted with knowledge of falsity or reckless disregard of truth or falsity. This rule has had a catastrophic effect upon defamation suits by police officers, for the reasons described below.

(i) *Police Officers Are "Public Officials."* It has been consistently held that police officers are public officials. This applies not only to high-ranking officers but also to ordinary patrolmen and all ranks in between.[70]

(ii) *Police Plaintiffs Must Show "Malice."* Because police officers are public officials, they cannot recover for defamation unless they can show "malice" in the *New York Times* sense — *i.e.,* knowledge of falsity or reckless disregard of truth or falsity.[71] This type of "malice" is never presumed; the burden is upon the plaintiff officer to establish such "malice" with "convincing clarity." [72] *Intent to harm is not sufficient by itself to establish "malice,"*[73] nor is it enough to show mere negligence, failure to investigate, or errors in judgment.[74]

Appellate courts have frequently reversed favorable trial court verdicts on the grounds that there was insufficient evidence of "malice," or that the court failed to instruct the jury properly on the necessity of showing "malice." [75]

Counsel should also be aware that *several cases have resulted in summary judgment for the defendant on the grounds that a bare allegation of "malice" in the pleadings is not enough to sustain the action.*[76] Enough detailed information must be provided in the pleadings to raise a fact question as to the existence of "malice" if the plaintiff is to avoid an adverse summary judgment.[77]

Even if the officer cannot establish actual knowledge of falsity, he may win by showing reckless disregard of truth or falsity. Even this, however, can be difficult. It requires a showing that the defendant must have entertained "serious doubts" as to the truth of the statements.[78] However, evidence of refusal to retract is admissible to show reckless disregard.[79]

Since *New York Times,* few police plaintiff defamation cases have survived the attention of the appellate courts. Exceptions, in which judgments have been affirmed by higher courts, include *Mahnke v. Northwest Publications, Inc.*[80] (evidence of malice sufficient, $4,000 verdict affirmed), and *Tucker v. Kilgore,*[81] which held that the *New York Times* rule does not apply *where the statements are directed not at the official conduct or capacity of the officer but at his qualities as a man.*

(iii) *Retraction.* Retraction is not normally a complete defense. The officer may usually maintain a suit despite the retraction. However, statutes may require a demand for retraction as a prerequisite to filing suit.[82] As noted above, the officer may also show a failure to retract as evidence of "malice." [83]

(iv) *Bad Reputation of the Officer.* As noted earlier, the fact that the officer already had a bad reputation does not bar the action. It does, however, bear on the question of how much damage has actually been suffered due to the defendant's acts, and evidence of the officer's bad reputation is therefore admissible in court on that issue.[84]

(v) *The Citizen's Right to Complain.* In 1886, a newspaper defended a deputy sheriff's defamation suit on the grounds that by exposing the official's conduct the defendant newspaper was doing a public good. The court rejected the claim that this gave rise to any privilege, stating that what was being claimed as a public good was in fact a public injury.[85] Today, however, not only have the courts taken a different view of the function of the press, as manifested by the *New York Times* decision and its multiple offspring, but, in addition, some courts at least have summarily dismissed or reversed defamation cases involving citizen complaints against police officers on the grounds that a citizen has, in effect, a privilege to complain about the manner in which he has been treated by the police, and cannot be sued for such complaints.[86] This general attitude is discussed in more detail in Chapter 10.

g. Summary.

In short, police officers now have a very difficult road ahead when they file defamation actions. Those that survive summary judgment and the tender mercies of the jury will often come to grief at the appellate level. In the appellate cases studied, the appellate court found in favor of the defendant in about two cases out of every three. Furthermore, of the few appellate decisions favoring the plaintiff officer, most involved only a remand on interim procedural points (such as summary judgment or demurrer) and did not involve affirmation of a final verdict in the officer's favor.

Results at the trial level are somewhat more often favorable; apparently juries are more sympathetic to police officers than judges are. Nevertheless, the actions of the trial judge often prevent the officer from even submitting his case to the jury, as in the case of dismissal or summary judgment.

Consequently, officers planning to bring defamation actions should look for a favorable settlement before trial or be prepared to carry a heavy burden of proof in the trial courts and to face the hostility of the appellate courts.

Until the pendulum of social and legal attitude swings again, defamation will probably continue to be the most difficult tort action for an officer to maintain.[87]

B. FALSE COMPLAINTS

Some of the cases encountered in the research for this book suggest that there is a separate cause of action for false complaints made by the defendant to the officer's departmental superiors — IAD, the Chief, etc.

Certainly, a false complaint can be the basis of a civil suit, but, properly speaking, there is no separate tort involved. Such complaints, when civilly actionable at all, are usually either defamation or malicious prosecution or both. Attempts to develop a separate form of action for false complaints will probably be of little benefit to police officers, because the doctrines of qualified privilege discussed above will still apply, and, as noted earlier, there is a substantial body of

162

judicial and lay opinion which would deny or at least limit the officer's right to sue for citizen complaints.

At present, such complaints are most often being treated as defamation and, despite the privilege problem, malice is perhaps more often and more easily proven in these cases than in those involving the news media, who seem to enjoy a virtual immunity from suit at the present time because of the courts' obsession with "freedom of the press."

A false complaint may be a crime as well as a tort. State statutes frequently make the filing of false reports or information a misdemeanor, and false allegations made to an internal affairs division have been construed as falling within the prohibition of such a statute.[88]

C. INTERFERENCE WITH THE EMPLOYMENT RELATIONSHIP

One possible source of additional assistance for the police officer who has been the victim of false complaints should be mentioned. In recent years there has been increasing recognition of a right of tort action where someone has intentionally interfered with the economic relationships of the plaintiff. The action may be available where the defendant has deliberately interfered with a contractual relationship, an employment relationship, or even the plaintiff's prospects of future economic advantage.[89]

The action is called by different names in different states, and may not even be recognized in all jurisdictions. Nevertheless, it is a separate and distinct tort remedy which should be investigated and considered in any situation in which some person has maliciously agitated to have an officer disciplined or discharged. It has the advantage of not (as yet at least) being subject to the *New York Times* rule; it appears that all that needs to be shown is that the interference was "intentional" in the sense of being

163

deliberate rather than negligent, and that the defendant acted for an improper purpose. Even where the defendant claims a privilege to interfere with the employment of a public officer on the grounds that the interference serves the public interest, this claim should be defeated by a showing that the defendant nevertheless acted primarily out of personal spite or ill-will, and beyond question the tort action should be successful where the statements made were known to be false.[90]

Therefore, in cases where an action for defamation will not be feasible because the statements made do not fit within the definition of defamation, or because of the strictures of the *New York Times* rule, or where the tort of malicious prosecution cannot be shown due to lack of one or more of the elements of that complex action, the officer may wish to explore the possibility, even if only as a last resort, that an action may be maintained for interference with the employment relationship.[91]

CHAPTER 8 — NOTES

1. Defamatory statements on radio or television may be slander or libel, depending upon statute or court decision in a particular jurisdiction.

2. *See also* 50 AM. JUR. 2d *Libel and Slander* § 1 (1970) (". . . must tend to lower the plaintiff in the opinion of men whose standard of opinion the court can properly recognize, or tend to induce them to entertain an ill opinion of him.") There are many other formulas used by the courts. In addition, there may be a statutory definition. *See* Coots v. Payton, 365 Mo. 180, 280 S.W.2d 47 (1955), citing Section 559.410 of the Missouri Code (". . . hatred, contempt or ridicule, or to deprive him of the benefits of public confidence and social intercourse . . . ").

3. Formerly it was not necessary to show actual damage for slander of the types about to be described; damages were "presumed." This appears to have been changed by Gertz v. Robert Welch, Inc., 418 U.S. 323, 94 S. Ct. 2997, 41 L. Ed. 2d 789 (1974) (not a police case), which states that there can be no recovery in defamation without some actual damage.

4. A few jurisdictions may require a showing of *special* damages if the libel is not apparent from the words themselves, but becomes plain only when the person reading the words is aware of certain extrinsic facts.

5. *Gertz,* note 3 *supra.*

6. *Gertz,* note 3 *supra.*

7. The absolute privilege of governmental officials is sometimes referred to as an "immunity" but the protection accorded to such officials in defamation actions is more properly called "privilege."

8. 376 U.S. 254, 84 S. Ct. 710, 11 L. Ed. 2d 686 (1964).

9. Curtis Publishing Co. v. Butts, 388 U.S. 130, 87 S. Ct. 1975, 18 L. Ed. 2d 1094, *rehearing denied,* 389 U.S. 889, 87 S. Ct. 1975, 18 L. Ed. 2d 1094 (1967).

10. For more detailed coverage, *see, e.g.,* PROSSER, LAW OF TORTS Ch. 21 (4th ed. 1971); *Recovery for Public Official Plaintiffs in Defamation,* THE POLICE PLAINTIFF, 77-3, at 9; and Blunt, *A Law Enforcement Officer Sues for Defamation,* FBI LAW ENFORCEMENT BULL., Feb. 1974.

11. As to defamation generally, *see* PROSSER, LAW OF TORTS § 111 *et seq.* (4th ed. 1971); and 50 AM. JUR. 2d *Libel and Slander* (1970).

12. While the following is not statistically reliable because of the small size of the sample, it is interesting to note that nearly 50% of the police plaintiff cases in the author's files at the time of this writing include a count in defamation.

13. Afro-American Publishing Co. v. Rudbeck, 101 App. D.C. 333, 248 F.2d 655 (D.C. Cir. 1957); Dill v. Rader, 533 P.2d 650 (Okla. App. 1975); Imig v. Ferrar, 70 Cal. App. 3d 48, 138 Cal. Rptr. 540 (1977); Jackson v.

Filliben, 281 A.2d 604 (Del. 1971); Suchomel v. Suburban Life Newspapers, Inc., 40 Ill. 2d 32, 240 N.E.2d 1 (1968); Weber v. Woods, 31 Ill. App. 3d 122, 334 N.E.2d 857 (1975); Tucker v. Kilgore, 388 S.W.2d 112 (Ky. 1965).

14. Smith v. Utley, 92 Wis. 133, 65 N.W. 744 (1896); Henry v. Collins, 380 U.S. 356, 85 S. Ct. 992, 13 L. Ed. 2d 892 (1965); Snively v. Record Publishing Co., 185 Cal. 565, 198 P. 1 (1921); Waiman v. Bowler, 576 P.2d 268 (Mont. 1978).

15. Lawrence v. Fox, 357 Mich. 134, 97 N.W.2d 719 (1959).

16. *See* THE POLICE PLAINTIFF, 76-1, at 4.

17. Borreseau v. Detroit Evening Journal, Inc., 63 Mich. 425, 30 N.W. 376 (1886); Hirman v. Rogers, 257 N.W.2d 563 (Minn. 1977).

18. Smith v. Byrd, 225 Miss. 361, 83 So.2d 172 (1955).

19. Rowden v. Amick, 446 S.W.2d 849 (Mo. App. 1969).

20. Coots v. Payton, 365 Mo. 180, 280 S.W.2d 47 (1955).

21. Gilligan v. Farmer, 30 App. Div. 2d 26, 289 N.Y.S.2d 846 (1968).

22. Mahnke v. Northwest Publications, Inc., 280 Minn. 328, 160 N.W.2d 1 (1968); McCarney v. Des Moines Register & Tribune Co., 239 N.W.2d 152 (Iowa 1976).

23. Time, Inc. v. Pape, 401 U.S. 279, 91 S. Ct. 633, 28 L. Ed. 2d 45 (1971).

24. NAACP v. Moody, 350 So.2d 1365 (Miss. 1977).

25. Meiners v. Moriarty, 563 F.2d 343 (7th Cir. 1977) (counterclaim).

26. Hanzimanolis v. City of New York, 88 Misc. 2d 681, 388 N.Y.S.2d 826 (1976); Hirman v. Rogers, 257 N.W.2d 563 (Minn. 1977); Coursey v. Greater Niles Township Publishing Corp., 40 Ill. 2d 257, 239 N.E.2d 837 (1968).

27. Matassa v. Bel, 246 La. 294, 164 So.2d 332 (1964) (candidate for constable).

28. *See* Webb v. Sessions, 531 S.W.2d 211 (Tex. Civ. App. 1975). *See also* Los Angeles Fire & Police Protective League v. Rodgers, 7 Cal. App. 3d 419, 425, 86 Cal. Rptr. 623, 627 (1970) (dictum).

29. *Id.*

30. *E.g.*, Afro-American Publishing Co. v. Rudbeck, 101 App. D.C. 333, 248 F.2d 655 (D.C. Cir. 1957); Borreseau v. Detroit Evening Journal, Inc., 63 Mich. 425, 30 N.W. 376 (1886); Mahnke v. Northwest Publications, Inc., 280 Minn. 328, 160 N.W.2d 1 (1968); McCarney v. Des Moines Register & Tribune Co., 239 N.W.2d 152 (Iowa 1976); Smith v. Byrd, 83 So.2d 172 (Miss. 1955); Smith v. Utley, 92 Wis. 133, 65 N.W. 744 (1896); Suchomel v. Suburban Life Newspapers, Inc., 40 Ill. 2d 32, 240 N.E.2d 1 (1968); Webb v. Sessions, 531 S.W.2d 211 (Tex. Civ. App. 1975); Coursey v. Greater Niles Township Publishing Corp., 40 Ill. 2d 257, 239 N.E.2d 837 (1968); Lawrence v. Fox, 357 Mich. 134, 97 N.W.2d 719 (1959); Snively v. Record Publishing

Co., 185 Cal. 565, 198 P. 1 (1921); Matassa v. Bel, 246 La. 294, 164 So.2d 332 (1964).

31. Jackson v. Filliben, 281 A.2d 604 (Del. 1971); Henry v. Collins, 380 U.S. 356, 85 S. Ct. 992, 13 L. Ed. 2d 892 (1965); Meiners v. Moriarity, 563 F.2d 343 (7th Cir. 1977). These suits are usually based on a departmental complaint made by the arrestee about the officer's conduct during the arrest.

32. Rowden v. Amick, 446 S.W.2d 849 (Mo. App. 1969) (parking ticket).

33. Dill v. Rader, 533 P.2d 650 (Okla. App. 1975); Hanzimanolis v. City of New York, 88 Misc. 2d 681, 388 N.Y.S.2d 826 (1976); Hirman v. Rogers, 257 N.W.2d 563 (Minn. 1977).

34. St. Amant v. Thompson, 390 U.S. 727, 88 S. Ct. 1323, 20 L. Ed. 2d 262 (1968); Weber v. Woods, 31 Ill. App. 3d 122, 334 N.E.2d 857 (1975).

35. Gilligan v. Farmer, 30 App. Div. 2d 26, 289 N.Y.S.2d 846 (1968); NAACP v. Moody, 350 So.2d 1365 (Miss. 1977).

36. THE POLICE PLAINTIFF, 77-3, at 6.

37. Time, Inc. v. Pape, 401 U.S. 279, 91 S. Ct. 633, 28 L. Ed. 2d 45 (1971).

38. Weber v. Woods, 31 Ill. App. 3d 122, 334 N.E.2d 857 (1975).

39. Tucker v. Kilgore, 388 S.W.2d 112 (Ky. 1965).

40. Barto v. Felix, 378 A.2d 927 (Pa. Sup. 1977) (public defender); THE POLICE PLAINTIFF, 77-3, at 5.

41. THE POLICE PLAINTIFF, 77-1, at 6.

42. THE POLICE PLAINTIFF, 77-1, at 7 (Kiwanis Club).

43. *E.g.,* high government officials. *See* Defenses *infra.* Not all of the defendants in the cases cited above were found liable, of course.

44. *See, e.g.,* Coots v. Payton, 365 Mo. 180, 280 S.W.2d 47 (1955).

45. Mullins v. Brando, 13 Cal. App. 3d 409, 91 Cal. Rptr. 796 (1970), *cert. denied,* 403 U.S. 923, 91 S. Ct. 2231, 29 L. Ed. 2d 701 (1971).

46. *See* cases cited above for details of the statements sued for. Whether a particular statement is actionable may depend on the exact wording. *Compare* Mullins v. Thieriot, 19 Cal. App. 3d 302, 97 Cal. Rptr. 27 (1971) (language not actionable) *with* Mullins v. Brando, 13 Cal. App. 3d 409, 91 Cal. Rptr. 796 (1970) (same incident, language actionable).

47. Tucker v. Kilgore, 388 S.W.2d 112 (Ky. 1965). *Cf.* Waiman v. Bowler, 576 P.2d 268 (Mont. 1978) (calling chief "bully boy" not actionable).

48. Coots v. Payton, 365 Mo. 180, 280 S.W.2d 47 (1955).

49. Meiners v. Moriarity, 563 F.2d 343 (7th Cir. 1977); NAACP v. Moody, 350 So.2d 1365 (Miss. 1977).

50. Rowden v. Amick, 446 S.W.2d 849 (Mo. App. 1969).

51. Tucker v. Kilgore, 388 S.W.2d 112 (Ky. 1965).

52. *See, e.g.,* Snively v. Record Publishing Co., 185 Cal. 565, 198 P. 1 (1921) (reversed on another point). (But a minor mistake in a cartoon does

not make it actionable. La Rocca v. New York News, Inc., 156 N.J. Super. 59, 383 A.2d 451 (1978).)

53. Gilligan v. Farmer, 30 App. Div. 2d 26, 289 N.Y.S.2d 846 (1968).

54. Webb v. Sessions, 531 S.W.2d 211 (Tex. Civ. App. 1975). *See also* Mullins v. Brando, 13 Cal. App. 3d 409, 91 Cal. Rptr. 796 (1970); Pigg v. Ashley County Newspaper, Inc., 253 Ark. 756, 489 S.W.2d 17 (1973). The result may be otherwise if the department is small, *e.g.,* less than two dozen officers. or so; in that case, derogatory remarks about the department, or unidentified members of it, will tend to affect all members and will therefore be actionable in many (but not all) jurisdictions.

55. THE POLICE PLAINTIFF, 76-3, at 8.

56. Reported in THE POLICE PLAINTIFF, 77-4, at 4. (Settlement of $5 after defendant admitted in open court that the charges he had made against the officer were false.)

57. Snively v. Record Publishing Co., 185 Cal. 565, 198 P. 1 (1921).

58. Smith v. Byrd, 225 Miss. 361, 83 So.2d 172 (1955).

59. Snively v. Record Publishing Co., 185 Cal. 565, 198 P. 1 (1921).

60. Dill v. Rader, 533 P.2d 650 (Okla. App. 1975).

61. Manning v. McAllister, 454 S.W.2d 597 (Mo. App. 1970).

62. *See, e.g.,* Coursey v. Greater Niles Township Publishing Corp., 40 Ill. 2d 257, 239 N.E.2d 837 (1968); Snively v. Record Publishing Co., 185 Cal. 565, 198 P. 1 (1921).

63. Coursey v. Greater Niles Township Publishing Corp., 40 Ill. 2d 257, 239 N.E.2d 837 (1968); Snively v. Record Publishing Co., 185 Cal. 565, 198 P. 1 (1921); Tucker v. Kilgore, 388 S.W.2d 112 (Ky. 1965).

64. *E.g.,* La Rocca v. New York News, Inc., 156 N.J. Super. 59, 383 A.2d 451 (1978); Matassa v. Bel, 246 La. 294, 164 So.2d 332 (1964).

65. Lawrence v. Fox, 357 Mich. 134, 97 N.W.2d 719 (1959).

66. Hanzimanolis v. City of New York, 88 Misc. 2d 681, 388 N.Y.S.2d 826 (1976). *See* Ch. 10 *infra* for additional discussion and cases.

67. *See* Imig v. Ferrar, 70 Cal. App. 3d 48, 138 Cal. Rptr. 540 (1977) (absolute privilege based upon California statute, for statements made in the course of official proceedings); Stern v. United States Gypsum, Inc., 547 F.2d 1329 (7th Cir.), *cert. denied,* 434 U.S. 975, 98 S. Ct. 533, 54 L. Ed. 2d 467 (1977) (was not a defamation case, but held that there is a constitutionally-based absolute privilege to complain about the conduct of government employees, in this instance an IRS agent); and THE POLICE PLAINTIFF, 76-2, at 7 (libel action by police officers dismissed due to "fundamental right of redress of grievances" of citizen).

68. *See* Barto v. Felix, 378 A.2d 927 (Pa. Super. 1977) (public defender). *See also* THE POLICE PLAINTIFF, 77-1, at 6 (judge, who would be absolutely privileged for derogatory remarks in the courtroom, wrote a letter to the

county board of supervisors criticising the plaintiff officer); and Harris v. Harvey, 419 F. Supp. 30 (E.D. Wis. 1976) (racial slurs by judge, civil rights suit). *Cf.* Hopper v. Allen, 266 Cal. App. 2d 797, 72 Cal. Rptr. 435 (1968) (defendant police chief issued press releases giving his version of dispute with plaintiff, a former police captain; summary judgment for defendant affirmed).

69. 376 U.S. 254, 84 S. Ct. 710, 11 L. Ed. 2d 686 (1964).

70. *See, e.g.,* Snively v. Record Publishing Co., 185 Cal. 565, 198 P. 1 (1921); Henry v. Collins, 380 U.S. 356, 85 S. Ct. 992, 13 L. Ed. 2d 892 (1965) (chiefs); Time, Inc. v. Pape, 401 U.S. 279, 91 S. Ct. 633, 28 L. Ed. 2d 45 (1971) (deputy chief); Lawrence v. Fox, 357 Mich. 134, 97 N.W.2d 719 (1959) (deputy superintendent); Coursey v. Greater Niles Township Publishing Corp., 40 Ill. 2d 257, 239 N.E.2d 837 (1968) (patrolman); Cline v. Brown, 24 N.C. App. 209, 210 S.E.2d 446 (1974) (deputy sheriff); NAACP v. Moody, 350 So.2d (Miss. 1977) (highway patrolman). *See also* 19 A.L.R.3d 1361, § 5 (1968). This had in fact been the rule prior to the *New York Times* case, but the classification of police as public officials did not, prior to *New York Times,* present any great difficulty because no showing of actual malice was required. *See* Snively v. Record Publishing Co., 185 Cal. 565, 198 P. 1 (1921).

71. *E.g.,* Hirman v. Rogers, 257 N.W.2d 563 (Minn. 1977).

72. *Id.*

73. Henry v. Collins, 380 U.S. 356, 85 S. Ct. 992, 13 L. Ed. 2d 892 (1965); Rowden v. Amick, 446 S.W.2d 849 (Mo. App. 1969).

74. McCarney v. Des Moines Register & Tribune Co., 239 N.W.2d 152 (Iowa 1976); Hirman v. Rogers, 257 N.W.2d 563 (Minn. 1977); Weber v. Woods, 31 Ill. App. 3d 122, 334 N.E.2d 857 (1975). Thus, if the statements were made in good faith, there can be no liability for defamation of the officer. Dellinger v. Belk, 34 N.C. App. 488, 238 S.E.2d 788 (1977).

75. Hirman v. Rogers, 257 N.W.2d 563 (Minn. 1977) (insufficient evidence); Jackson v. Filliben, 281 A.2d 604 (Del. 1971) (insufficient evidence); NAACP v. Moody, 350 So.2d 1365 (Miss. 1977) (improper instruction); Meiners v. Moriarity, 563 F.2d 343 (7th Cir. 1977) (improper instruction).

76. *See, e.g.,* Suchomel v. Suburban Life Newspapers Inc., 40 Ill. 2d 32, 240 N.E.2d 1 (1968).

77. *See* Weber v. Woods, 31 Ill. App. 3d 122, 334 N.E.2d 857 (1975); Coursey v. Greater Niles Township Publishing Corp., 40 Ill. 2d 257, 239 N.E.2d 837 (1968); and Matassa v. Bel, 246 La. 294, 164 So.2d 332 (1964), in which the allegations were held sufficient to avoid dismissal or summary judgment. *Cf.* Time, Inc. v. Pape, 401 U.S. 279, 91 S. Ct. 633, 28 L. Ed. 2d 45 (1971).

78. St. Amant v. Thompson, 390 U.S. 727, 88 S. Ct. 1323, 20 L. Ed. 2d 262 (1968).

79. Mahnke v. Northwest Publications, Inc., 280 Minn. 328, 160 N.W.2d 1 (1968).

80. Mahnke v. Northwest Publications, Inc., 280 Minn. 328, 160 N.W.2d 1 (1968).

81. Tucker v. Kilgore, 388 S.W.2d 112 (Ky. 1965).

82. *E.g.,* N.C. CODE § 99-1(a). *See* THE POLICE PLAINTIFF, 77-4, at 5.

83. Mahnke v. Northwest Publications, Inc., 280 Minn. 328, 160 N.W.2d 1 (1968).

84. Snively v. Record Publishing Co., 185 Cal. 565, 198 P. 1 (1921).

85. Borreseau v. Detroit Evening Journal, Inc., 63 Mich. 425, 30 N.W. 376 (1886) (judgment for plaintiff reversed on other grounds).

86. THE POLICE PLAINTIFF, 76-2, at 7.

87. For additional material on defamation actions by police plaintiffs, *see* the feature articles in THE POLICE PLAINTIFF, 77-2 and 77-3; and Blunt, *A Law Enforcement Officer Sues for Defamation,* FBI LAW ENFORCEMENT BULL., Feb. 1974.

88. *See* State v. Pandozzi, 136 N.J. Super. 484, 347 A.2d 1 (1975).

89. *See* PROSSER, LAW OF TORTS §§ 129, 130 (4th ed. 1971).

90. *Id.*

91. In Meester v. Davies, 11 Cal. App. 3d 342, 89 Cal. Rptr. 711 (1970), a police chief brought action for tortious interference with contract and malicious prosecution. The complaint was rejected on procedural grounds by both the trial and appellate courts without discussion of the merits of the allegation of tortious interference with contract.

Chapter 9

ACTIONS FOR INVASION OF THE OFFICER'S CIVIL RIGHTS; INVASION OF PRIVACY; PROPERTY DAMAGE; OTHER ACTIONS

A. ACTIONS FOR INVASION OF THE OFFICER'S CIVIL RIGHTS

1. *General Considerations*

As every police officer is well aware, there has been a vast amount of civil litigation during recent years for alleged violations of civil rights. Many of these actions have involved police as defendants for alleged violations of the civil rights of arrestees and other citizens; little if any attention has been paid by the courts to the civil rights of the police officer.

Theoretically, at least, the individual law enforcement officer enjoys the same rights extended to the civilian citizen; there is no express language in the Constitution or the civil rights statutes which specifically denies rights to any person merely because that person happens to be a police officer.

Nevertheless, there is very little litigation by police plaintiffs involving claims of civil rights violations; and the bulk of the existing cases have involved officers bringing action against their own departments over employment-related matters, such as disciplinary procedures or discrimination in promotion practices. Actions by officers against third parties for violation of individual civil rights not related to internal matters are apparently extremely rare.

There are several reasons for this lack of assertion of constitutional and statutory civil rights.

1. The constitutional and statutory provisions establishing the civil rights of the citizen are, in the main, concerned with deprivation of rights by governmental action, and are not oriented toward redress of wrongs

171

committed by private persons. They were designed, in short, to protect private citizens from the police, and not to protect the police from private citizens.

2. Even those sections of the civil rights acts which do permit actions for deprivation of rights by the acts of private individuals are primarily concerned with class-based discrimination, *e.g.,* racial discrimination. They were for the most part simply not conceived or designed for use in situations in which no racial or other group-oriented discrimination is involved.

3. In view of the foregoing, the courts have quite naturally proceeded to interpret these various constitutional and statutory provisions in a manner which has left very little room for the use of these rights and remedies by the individual police officer in situations not involving internal employment matters. In fact, the courts have quite obviously leaned over backwards to interpret these laws in all respects in a manner which consistently favors the private citizen at the expense of police officers or other officials. Again, the intent is to protect the citizen against the police and not vice versa.

4. Finally, because attorneys are perfectly aware of the foregoing, there have been very few *attempts* to utilize civil rights — constitutional or statutory — as the basis for nonemployment litigation by police plaintiffs. Consequently, there is little precedent for civil rights actions by police officers outside the employment context, and this sheer lack of precedent itself discourages new attempts.

Nevertheless, the possibility of a civil rights action may be worth exploring in any situation in which the officer's attorney feels that the express language of the law gives any latitude for an interpretation favorable to the officer.

2. *The Civil Rights Acts*

Officers have so often been defendants in Civil Rights Act violation cases that a brief examination of the best-known provisions from the standpoint of the officer as a potential plaintiff under these sections may be of interest.

a. § 1981.

42 U.S.C. § 1981 provides:

> All persons within the jurisdiction of the United States shall have the same right in every State and Territory to make and enforce contracts, to sue, be parties, give evidence, and to the full and equal benefit of all laws and proceedings for the security of persons and property as is enjoyed by white citizens, and shall be subject to like punishment, pains, penalties, taxes, licenses, and exactions of every kind, and to no other.

Although this section has been construed to apply to private as well as governmental action, and can be the basis for a civil suit, it is, as the wording suggests, designed for (and limited to) situations involving racial discrimination.[1]

b. § 1983.

42 U.S.C. § 1983 states:

> Every person who, under color of any statute, ordinance, regulation, custom, or usage, of any State or Territory, subjects, or causes to be subjected, any citizen of the United States or other person within the jurisdiction thereof to the deprivation of any rights, privileges, or immunities secured by the Constitution and laws, shall be liable to the party injured in an action at law, suit in equity, or other proper proceeding for redress.

Actions under this section need not be based on racial discrimination; other constitutional and statutory rights are protected. However, the deprivation of rights complained of must be by official action; wrongs by private individuals not committed under color of law are not covered.

Since the concept of official action includes acts by municipal or police officials, police officers have used this section as a basis for suits over employment-related disputes,[2] but it is simply not designed to cover situations in which the officer has been injured by a private citizen.[3]

Where applicable, it provides a right of civil action in which a successful plaintiff may recover money damages, including punitive damages even where no actual damage is shown; injunctive relief; and attorneys' fees.[4]

c. § 1985.

42 U.S.C. § 1985 reads as follows:

(1) If two or more persons in any State or Territory conspire to prevent, by force, intimidation, or threat, any person from accepting or holding any office, trust, or place of confidence under the United States, or from discharging any duties thereof; or to induce by like means any officer of the United States to leave any State, district, or place, where his duties as an officer are required to be performed, or to injure him in his person or property on account of his lawful discharge of the duties of his office, or while engaged in the lawful discharge thereof, or to injure his property so as to molest, interrupt, hinder, or impede him in the discharge of his official duties;

(2) If two or more persons in any State or Territory conspire to deter, by force, intimidation, or threat, any party or witness in any court of the United States from attending such court, or from testifying to any matter pending therein, freely, fully, and truthfully, or to injure such party or witness in his person or property on account of his having so attended or testified, or to influence the verdict, presentment, or indictment of any grand or petit juror in any such court, or to injure such juror in his person or property on account of any verdict, presentment, or indictment lawfully assented to by

him, or of his being or having been such juror; or if two or more persons conspire for the purpose of impeding, hindering, obstructing, or defeating, in any manner, the due course of justice in any State or Territory, with intent to deny to any citizen the equal protection of the laws, or to injure him or his property for lawfully enforcing, or attempting to enforce, the right of any person, or class of persons, to the equal protection of the laws;

(3) If two or more persons in any State or Territory conspire or go in disguise on the highway or on the premises of another, for the purpose of depriving, either directly or indirectly, any person or class of persons of the equal protection of the laws, or of equal privileges and immunities under the laws; or for the purpose of preventing or hindering the constituted authorities of any State or Territory from giving or securing to all persons within such State or Territory the equal protection of the laws; or if two or more persons conspire to prevent by force, intimidation, or threat, any citizen who is lawfully entitled to vote, from giving his support or advocacy in a legal manner, toward or in favor of the election of any lawfully qualified person as an elector for President or Vice President, or as a Member of Congress of the United States; or to injure any citizen in person or property on account of such support or advocacy; in any case of conspiracy set forth in this section, if one or more persons engaged therein do, or cause to be done, any act in furtherance of the object of such conspiracy, whereby another is injured in his person or property, or deprived of having and exercising any right or privilege of a citizen of the United States, the party so injured or deprived may have an action for the recovery of damages, occasioned by such injury or deprivation, against any one or more of the conspirators.

This section does not require that there be any official action; wrongs by private persons are actionable. There must, however, be a *conspiracy* to violate the plaintiff's civil rights; the action of one person, not taken in conspiracy with others, is not covered.

The bulk of the litigation under this section has been brought under subsection (3), and the courts have repeatedly held that this subsection does not apply to all tortious conspiracies,[5] but only to those directed at depriving the plaintiff of the equal protection of the laws or the privileges and immunities enjoyed by other citizens.[6] There must, therefore, be an element of *class discrimination* for the conspiracy to be actionable under this subsection.[7]

Again, where applicable, punitive damages, injunctive relief, and attorneys' fees may be awarded to the prevailing plaintiff.[8]

Because of the interpretations placed upon this subsection, it would appear, again, that it will be difficult to apply to the normal police plaintiff case.

Subsection (1) of the statute, prohibiting conspiracies to impede federal officers in the performance of their duties, appears to have potential usefulness for federal law enforcement officers. The section prohibits conspiracies by private persons; the conspiracy need not be motivated by "discriminatory animus"; and the duties impeded need not relate to the Fourteenth Amendment.[9] Nevertheless, a U.S. Court of Appeals and the Supreme Court of the United States have rejected an attempt by an internal revenue agent to recover damages under this section.[10]

d. §§ 1986, 1988.

42 U.S.C. § 1986 (neglect or refusal to prevent § 1985 violation) and 42 U.S.C. § 1988 (jurisdiction and attorneys' fees) may also be relevant. See below.

176

3. Actions by Police Plaintiffs Under the Federal Civil Rights Acts

Two cases brought by police plaintiffs under sections of the federal Civil Rights Acts illustrate the problems involved for the officer contemplating a civil rights suit.

In *Taylor v. Nichols*,[11] the plaintiff was a city policeman who had been charged with criminal assault and battery by an 18-year-old arrestee who openly threatened to "get (the plaintiff's) badge." The plaintiff was suspended pending trial. After being found not guilty of the charges against him, the officer filed a civil rights action under 42 U.S.C. §§ 1983, 1985, 1986, and 1988 against the arrestee, the arrestee's father, the arrestee's attorney (who had been appointed special prosecutor to bring criminal charges against the officer), the county attorney, the county judge, and three members of the board of commissioners of the county. The plaintiff alleged that the defendants acted in concert under color of law and conspired to deprive him of his constitutional rights because of "his lawful discharge of the duties of his office as a policeman."

The federal judge who heard the defendant's motion to dismiss held that "the complaint failed to allege a colorable deprivation of any rights secured by the Constitution or laws of the United States" and dismissed the officer's action.

In dismissing the suit, the court made the following observations:

> a. The Civil Rights Acts does not provide a remedy for mere common-law torts, even when committed under color of state law. Therefore, libel or slander, or injury to reputation due to criminal prosecution, even when committed by state officials acting maliciously, are not covered by the Civil Rights Acts; and allegations of mental distress, harassment, and injury to person and

property due to the criminal prosecution are likewise not actionable under the Acts.

b. Anti-police bias, or discrimination against the plaintiff solely because he was a policeman, is not the sort of class-based discrimination prohibited by the Civil Rights Acts.

c. "Conclusory allegations" of violations of constitutional rights, unsupported by specifics, are not sufficient to state a cause of action under federal law.

The court concluded that: "While this allegation might state a classic claim for relief under the tort theories relating to malicious prosecution, it is not justiciable under the Civil Rights Act." [12]

In this court's view, then, discrimination against police officers as a class is not actionable under the Civil Rights Act.

By contrast, in *Harris v. Harvey,*[13] in which a black police lieutenant filed an action against a local judge for alleged racial slurs against the plaintiff, the federal court ruled that:

a. The judge's judicial immunity did not cover the acts complained of;

b. The plaintiff had adequately alleged a violation of rights cognizable under the act; and

c. The plaintiff was entitled to bring the case to trial.

The court therefore refused to dismiss the suit.

The difference in result in these two cases, in both of which the gist of the complaint was injury to reputation, is an excellent illustration of the point made earlier herein about the underlying purpose and original intent of the Civil Rights Acts. Unless racial discrimination is involved, the Acts simply are not regarded by the courts as being for the benefit of police officers as a class. Except for employment cases and cases of the type filed by Lt. Harris, the federal Civil Rights Acts will be of limited value to police officers — at least until the federal courts can be persuaded to interpret the acts more broadly.

4. State Statutes; Police "Bills of Rights"; State Civil Rights Commissions

Some states have granted special statutory rights to police officers. Occasionally these have been offered to the legislatures in the form of a package "Police Bill of Rights." Enactment of these statutes has been, for the most part, on a piecemeal basis, and most of the enactments have dealt with such matters as employment rights, pay and fringe benefits, and pension plans. These matters are, of course, beyond the scope of this book.

In a few states, the "Police Bill of Rights" makes specific reference to the right of law enforcement officers to bring civil suits for violations of their civil rights or other injuries suffered in the line of duty.[14] For the most part, however, tort remedies of police officers have been left to the dictates of the common law and whatever statutes govern tort actions by all citizens.

Nevertheless, counsel should consult the code of the particular jurisdiction to determine if the legislature has in any way modified or expanded the rights of action of police officers in that jurisdiction for torts by third persons.

In some instances, the state will have a special agency set up to handle civil rights violation complaints. Police officers may be able to obtain some form of redress through these agencies, particularly if class discrimination is involved.[15]

5. Summary

In summary, it appears that there has been little attempt to utilize statutory or constitutional civil rights guarantees by police officers outside of employment disputes, and any attempt to employ the existing laws in any other context on

179

behalf of the police plaintiff will meet with substantial difficulties.

Despite this, perhaps more attention should be paid to this avenue of potential recovery. Vigorous employment of the express language of the civil rights acts, coupled with continued assertion of the position that "police officers are people too," may serve to call to the attention of the courts the manner in which the rights of the police officer have been neglected, and, perhaps, to induce at least some courts to conclude that those who are obligated to enforce our laws are also entitled to be protected by them.

B. INVASION OF PRIVACY

1. *General Considerations*

Under certain circumstances, a police officer (and perhaps the officer's family) may have a right of action for invasion of the officer's privacy. Four types of right of privacy actions are generally recognized in this country today. They are usually identified as follows:

    a. Appropriation of name or likeness.

    b. Intrusion upon physical or mental solitude.

    c. Public disclosure of private facts.

    d. Presenting the plaintiff to the public in a false light.[16]

The first type covers unauthorized use of a person's name, picture, etc., in endorsements of commercial products, and appears to have little application in the law enforcement context.

The second type of action, intrusion upon solitude, might be applicable in any situation where, for example, electronic listening devices have been used unlawfully to eavesdrop in the officer's home, or a tap has been placed on his telephone.

The third type, public disclosure of private facts, may be useful to the officer in situations where intimate or embarrassing details of the officer's past life have been made public without justification, for example, as part of an anti-police or anti-officer campaign on the part of an underground newspaper. The advantage here is that the action can be maintained *even though the statements are true.* Thus, the remedy is available in situations where defamation actions are not possible.

The fourth type of privacy action, presentation of the plaintiff in a false light, more closely resembles defamation in that the element of falsity must be present. This action is available in cases where the statements involved are not sufficiently flagrant to constitute libel or slander, but which nevertheless give the public an erroneous impression about the plaintiff. For example, an erroneous report that the officer was overpowered by a prisoner would probably not be actionable as libel or slander, but might be the subject of a right of privacy action because a false image of the officer's experience was presented to the public.[17]

A potential stumbling block to the use by police personnel of right of privacy suits is the likelihood that the courts will regard the plaintiff officer as a public official, or at least as a public or "newsworthy" figure. This presents difficulties, because even at common law news media have a right to report on "newsworthy" events and persons, which would normally include the commission of a crime and the people involved in it. To the extent that the officer has become "newsworthy," therefore, the right of privacy may be lost or at least severely limited. Furthermore, the Supreme Court has extended coverage of the rule of the case of *New York Times v. Sullivan* (discussed above in connection with defamation) to include right of privacy actions.[18]

2. *Right of Privacy Actions by Police Plaintiffs*

Relatively little use has been made of the right of privacy action by police officers. This is probably due in part to lack of familiarity with the tort, in part to the fact that not all jurisdictions recognize the right fully, and, to some degree at least, to the application of the *New York Times* rule to privacy cases and the current emphasis in the courts on unbridled "freedom of the press."

For example, in 1975, the Court of Appeals of New Mexico considered a right of privacy action brought by five police officers and their families against a newspaper which had printed the names and addresses of the officers in connection with a story about a gun battle with a militant group. The officers alleged that this action, allegedly done maliciously in retaliation for the officers' refusal to supply the newspaper's city editor with details of the shooting, resulted in anonymous threatening phone calls being received by the officers and their families. The plaintiffs contended that this constituted an intrusion upon their solitude and public disclosure of private facts. (See general discussion of right of privacy, above.) The court, acknowledging that the right of privacy, or "right to be let alone," was recognized in New Mexico, went on to hold that (1) the publication of the officers' names and addresses was not an actionable invasion of privacy, and (2) even if it was an invasion of privacy, it was *privileged* because it was *"newsworthy."* The court said:

> ... One of the key qualifications to the right is where the individual's right of privacy conflicts with the first amendment's freedom of the press. In such a circumstance, the individual's right of privacy must yield to the greater public interest in the dissemination of newsworthy material.[19]

Other courts have held flatly that no right of privacy exists as to any inquiry into the police officer's discharge of the officer's public duties. An Illinois appellate court has stated:

> In our opinion, the very status of the policeman as a public official ... is tantamount to an implied consent to informing the general public by all legitimate means regarding his activities in discharge of his public duties.[20]

This view would seem to preclude right of privacy actions by officers in most instances where the invasion of privacy was directed at gathering information about the officer's performance of his duty, especially where the defendant is a part of the news media. This would, in effect, eliminate the possibility of recovery in the majority of right-of-privacy actions by officers.[21]

Nevertheless, a few privacy actions by police plaintiffs have been successful, at least at the trial level. In one case, two officers reportedly obtained judgments against members of a police corruptions unit which had been investigating the plaintiff officers. The plaintiffs alleged that during the course of this investigation, the officers of the police corruptions unit had strip-searched the plaintiff policemen in a parking lot, arrested them, and searched them again. The plaintiffs filed an action in the United States District Court for the Northern District of Illinois for invasion of privacy, and were awarded $17,000 each by the jury.[22]

In another case, a former police officer has reportedly obtained a $70,000 judgment against the city of Seattle for actions of police investigators taken in connection with the plaintiff's disability claim. The investigators allegedly questioned the plaintiff's neighbors and videotaped him without his knowledge. The action was reported as being based upon "harassment," but it appears to be grounded upon conduct and principles applicable to right of privacy actions.[23]

In summary, it appears that right of privacy actions by police officers are possible, but that where the case involves an inquiry by the news media into the officer's official activities, recovery will be difficult if not impossible.[24]

3. *Right of Privacy Actions by the Officer's Family*

An additional consideration for the officer is the fact that many invasions of the officer's privacy will involve an invasion of the privacy of the other members of the officer's family as well. The wiretap or the listening device in the bedroom, for example, may constitute an invasion of the privacy of every member of the family, and every family member whose privacy has been invaded will have a right of action for that invasion. Multiple actions will, of course, multiply the chances of recovery and increase the total potential recovery.

Furthermore, defenses which may prevent the police officer from recovery *may* not be applicable to suits by other members of the family, and juries may display more sympathy for a civilian whose privacy has been invaded than would be shown to an officer making the same complaint.[25]

C. PROPERTY DAMAGE

1. *General Considerations*

The majority of litigation by police officers — and therefore the majority of this book — is concerned with injuries to person or reputation. The possibility of a right of action for damage to the officer's personal or real property should not be overlooked, however. In many instances, of course, claims for property damage will accompany personal injuries and will be litigated in the same action as the personal injury claims. Nevertheless, several different rights of action for personal injury has been suffered and without reference to any other form of action or element of damages.

2. *Negligent Damage to Property*

Where real or personal property of an officer has been damaged through the carelessness of some other person, a negligence action will lie and the principles involved are identical to those applicable in personal injury cases, discussed earlier. In this context, the term "damage" also includes destruction or loss of the property.

3. *Intentional Damage to Property*

Where the officer's property has been deliberately damaged by someone, there are at least three possible intentional tort remedies which can be employed.

a. Trespass to Land.

Trespass to land is the appropriate form of action where real estate has been unlawfully entered or damaged by the defendant. The action is available against any person who sets foot upon the property or intentionally causes some object to be propelled onto the property. Therefore, where someone comes into an officer's yard without permission, or, even without entering onto the property, throws rocks at the windows or tosses garbage into the yard, the action can be maintained. No actual damage need be shown; punitive damages may be available.

b. Trespass to Chattels.

Trespass to chattels is one of the forms of action available when personal property has been damaged. This action, which is used relatively little today, is nonetheless proper where there is relatively minor but intentional (not negligent) damage to or interference with personal property (chattels) of the officer. This remedy might be appropriate where, for example, an officer's personal vehicle has been vandalized

185

or a pet animal belonging to the officer or a member of the officer's family has been deliberately wounded or poisoned.

Unlike most of the intentional torts, trespass to chattels requires a showing of actual damage (no nominal damages permitted), but here "actual damage" includes deprivation of the use of the chattel as well as physical damage to the chattel, and even the slightest damage is sufficient to support the action, in which event punitive damages may be recoverable as well.

c. Conversion.

Where there has been serious damage to or deprivation of the use of the chattel, the more common tort remedy today is the action of conversion. Conversion is also an intentional tort, meaning that the action can be maintained only where there has been deliberate interference with or damage to the chattel. Conversion is, in a sense, the tort equivalent of larceny; a conversion action will lie in virtually any situation in which the defendant could be charged with the crime of larceny. Theft of an officer's revolver would therefore be conversion, for example.

Conversion includes much more than just larceny, however. The action can be brought even though there was no intent to deprive the owner of the chattel permanently. It is the proper action where the damage has been so severe that the chattel has been effectively ruined, or where it has been totally destroyed. If, for example, an officer's vehicle were set afire and destroyed, the proper remedy would be a conversion action.

The measure of compensatory damages in a conversion action is normally the fair market value of the chattel at the time of the conversion; punitive damages may be available also.[26]

4. *Property Damage Actions by Police Plaintiffs*

There is virtually no information currently available from central sources about property damage actions by police plaintiffs. Where property damage occurs, it is often claimed in connection with a suit for personal injuries or other torts rather than in a separate action, so that it is difficult to identify the property damage aspect of the case in research indices; and, in addition, lower court cases involving only property damage are unlikely to receive the publicity accorded to personal injury actions (where the drama — and the judgments — will normally be much greater).

Nevertheless, officers may find property damage claims of benefit in the following situations:

a. The officer may include a claim for any property damage suffered when filing an action for any other tort discussed in this book. For example, in a battery action for ripping off the officer's badge, the cost of repairing or replacing the badge or shirt may be asserted as an element of damages.

b. Where no other legally protected right has been invaded, the officer may nevertheless wish to bring a separate action — *e.g.*, for vandalism of the officer's personal motor vehicle.

c. Even where there is no actual damage, as in a technical trespass to land, the availability of the remedy may be helpful to establish a precedent or to bring the weight of the law to bear on antagonists who are otherwise beyond reach. Thus, for example, any person coming upon the officer's property without the consent of the officer is liable for trespass; therefore, where someone has entered the officer's yard or home for some purpose such as harassment or an attempt to harm the officer or the officer's family, but proof of the more serious criminal or civil offense is lacking, a simple action

187

for trespass to land may serve to produce a substantial judgment, including punitive damages.

D. OTHER ACTIONS

In these pages, specific tort actions have been considered, many in great detail.

Two points should be noted:

1. There are other forms of tort action which, while not mentioned here and not heretofore employed by police plaintiffs, may be of use in a particular case. Counsel should not hesitate to utilize *any* form of action, whether discussed here or not, which appears to be applicable in a given situation.

2. Many states do not now require that the complaint be labeled as any specific form of action. The plaintiff may be able simply to state what occurred without being forced to try to fit the case into any legal pigeonhole. Nevertheless, it will usually be found that there can be no recovery unless the conduct complained of meets the requirements of one of the forms of action recognized at common law. Consequently, the liberalization of the rules of pleading does not necessarily relieve the plaintiff of the task of determining which — if any — of the common-law torts have been committed.

The ultimate key to recovery will continue to be the ingenuity and aggressiveness of plaintiff and plaintiff's counsel.

CHAPTER 9 — NOTES

1. *See* 42 U.S.C.A. § 1981 and annotations thereto; 15 AM. JUR. 2d *Civil Rights* §§ 12-13 (1976).

2. *See, e.g.,* Fitzgerald v. Cawley, 368 F. Supp. 677 (S.D.N.Y. 1973) (New York City patrolmen v. New York City police commissioner); D'Iorio v. County of Delaware, 447 F. Supp. 229 (E.D. Pa. 1978) (County detective v. county, county council, and district attorney); Detroit Police Officers Ass'n v. Young, 446 F. Supp. 979 (E.D. Mich. 1978) (police association v. mayor, chief of police, and others).

3. *See,* however, Harris v. Harvey, 419 F. Supp. 30 (E.D. Wis. 1976), discussed in Section 3 *infra.*

4. *E.g.,* 42 U.S.C.A. § 1983 and annotations thereto; 15 AM. JUR. 2d *Civil Rights* §§ 16-21 (1976).

5. *E.g.,* Cohen v. Illinois Inst. of Tech., 524 F.2d 818 (7th Cir. 1975), *cert. denied,* 425 U.S. 943, 96 S. Ct. 1683, 48 L. Ed. 2d 187 (1976) (not a police case).

6. Doski v. M. Goldseker Co., 539 F.2d 1326 (4th Cir. 1976) (not a police case).

7. McNally v. Pulitzer Publishing Co., 532 F.2d 69 (8th Cir.), *cert. denied,* 429 U.S. 855, 97 S. Ct. 150, 50 L. Ed. 2d 131 (1976) (not a police case). *See also* Taylor v. Nichols, 409 F. Supp. 927 (D. Kan. 1976), *aff'd,* 558 F.2d 561 (10th Cir. 1977), discussed in Section 3 *infra.*

8. *See* 42 U.S.C.A. § 1985 and annotations thereto; 15 AM. JUR. *Civil Rights* § 25 (1976).

9. Stern v. United States Gypsum, Inc., 547 F.2d 1329 (7th Cir.), *cert. denied,* 434 U.S. 975, 98 S. Ct. 533, 54 L. Ed. 2d 467 (1977) (stating principles but denying recovery on other grounds) (*see* note 10 *infra*).

10. *Id.* The plaintiff alleged that the defendants had tried to impede an audit by filing a false complaint against him. The court denied recovery on grounds that there is a constiutional right to complain to higher authority about the conduct of government employees. *See* Ch. 8 *supra* and Ch. 10 *infra* for further discussion of this "right to complain."

11. 409 F. Supp. 927 (D. Kan. 1976), *aff'd,* 558 F.2d 561 (10th Cir. 1977).

12. 409 F. Supp. 927, 937 (D. Kan. 1976), *aff'd,* 558 F.2d 561 (10th Cir. 1977).

13. 419 F. Supp. 30 (E.D. Wis. 1976).

14. *E.g.,* FLA. STAT. § 112.532 (3), which provides that "[e]very law enforcement officer shall have the right to bring civil suit . . . for damages . . . suffered during the performance of the officer's official duties or for abridgment of the officer's civil rights. . . ." (The validity of this section was upheld in Mesa v. Rodriguez, 357 So.2d 711 (Fla. 1978).)

189

15. Two New York police officers reportedly filed complaints with the New York State Division of Human Rights when a restaurant owner refused to serve them because they were in uniform. *See* The POLICE PLAINTIFF, 76-3, at 4.

16. PROSSER, LAW OF TORTS Ch. 20 (4th ed. 1971).

17. For additional information about the right of privacy, *see, e.g.,* PROSSER, LAW OF TORTS Ch. 20 (4th ed. 1971); and 62 AM. JUR. 2d *Privacy* (1972).

18. Time, Inc. v. Hill, 385 U.S. 374, 87 S. Ct. 534, 17 L. Ed. 2d 456 (1967).

19. McNutt v. New Mexico State Tribune Co., 88 N.M. 162, 538 P.2d 804, 808 (N.M. App. 1975), *cert. denied,* 540 P.2d 248 (1975) (citing *New York Times v. Sullivan*).

20. Cassidy v. American Broadcasting Co., 60 Ill. App. 3d 831, 377 N.E.2d 126 (1978). *See also* Rawlins v. Hutchinson Publishing Co., 218 Kan. 295, 543 P.2d 988 (1975).

21. For additional cases involving surreptitious taping or filming of an officer's activities, *see* THE POLICE PLAINTIFF, 76-2, at 10, and 76-4, at 7.

22. THE POLICE PLAINTIFF, 76-4, at 7. (Note that the defendants in this case were *not* representatives of the news media.)

23. THE POLICE PLAINTIFF, 78-1, at 8. (Note that the defendants in this case were *not* representatives of the news media, and that the case did *not* involve the (former) officer's official duties.)

24. Some invasions of privacy, such as illegal wiretapping, may of course also carry criminal penalties.

25. *Cf.* McNutt v. New Mexico State Tribune Co., note 19 *supra,* in which members of the officers' families joined in the action as plaintiffs without success.

26. For additional discussion of property damage actions, *see* PROSSER, LAW OF TORTS Ch. 3 (4th ed. 1971); and 18 AM. JUR. 2d *Conversion* (1965) and 75 AM. JUR. 2d *Trespass* (1974).

Part IV
PRACTICAL CONSIDERATIONS

Chapter 10

OBSTACLES TO RECOVERY

A. LEGAL OBSTACLES

Some of the technical defenses and other legal obstacles confronting the police plaintiff have been pointed out in connection with each form of action. Now, a summary and overview may be helpful.

1. Defenses

a. Assumption of the Risk, Consent, Contributory Negligence.

The legal defenses of assumption of the risk, consent, and contributory negligence are standard defenses in tort actions generally. Naturally, defendants in police plaintiff cases may be expected to attempt to raise them.

The defense of "assumption of the risk" may be a serious problem in police plaintiff cases. Although the officer does not, by deciding to become a police officer, or by doing his duty as a police officer, automatically assume all of the numerous risks involved in the profession, there are at least two types of cases where assumption of the risk or related concepts have often been invoked to bar the officer's recovery. These are (1) premises defects cases and (2) cases in which the officer is suing a third party for negligently creating, or permitting to exist, the conditions which led to an intentional assault by a third person.[1] These problems are discussed in Chapter 5.

Some courts apparently view assumption of the risk as an absolute defense in *all* police plaintiff negligence cases, due to the "inherent danger" of the law officer's profession.

Consent, which is the intentional tort counterpart of the negligence doctrine of assumption of risk, has not apparently

193

been quite as much of a problem; for example, no case has been found in which it has been successfully contended that by becoming a police officer the plaintiff expressly or impliedly consented to be assaulted or battered regardless of the circumstances of the attack.

Contributory negligence is always available as a defense in negligence actions if the officer has, under the facts of the particular case, failed to behave as the ordinary prudent officer would have behaved, and this defense has often been raised in automobile accident cases. Generally, it is not contributory negligence to do your duty, and therefore arguments that, *e.g.,* the officer was contributorily negligent simply because he was engaged in a high speed pursuit, have not usually impressed the courts. However, if the duty was done in an improper manner, as, for example, where the officer's actions violate statutes, ordinances, or departmental procedures, this may lead to a finding of contributory negligence which will bar or greatly reduce the officer's recovery.[2] This problem is also discussed in Chapter 5.

b. Privilege.

Where the basis of the suit is the defendant's public criticism of the officer's official capacity or conduct, the constitutional privilege announced in the case of *New York Times v. Sullivan* [3] will prevent recovery by the officer unless it can be shown that the defendant acted with knowledge of falsity or reckless disregard of truth or falsity.[4]

In addition, some courts, accepting an argument frequently heard from defense attorneys and others, have apparently recognized a so-called "right to complain" of the conduct of the police, which, depending on the court, may amount to a qualified or even an absolute privilege.[5] In a recent case, *Stern v. United States Gypsum, Inc.,* the Seventh Circuit Court of Appeals denied recovery to an IRS agent who had sued under the Civil Rights Act, 42 U.S.C. § 1985

(1), for a complaint made against him to his superiors by defendants whom the agent was auditing. The court stated that the First Amendment to the Constitution of the United States applies to complaints presented to responsible government officials about the conduct of subordinate government employees, and that this constitutional protection prevents a finding of liability under the statute in question *even if the complaint was knowingly false.*[6]

These cases, which imply or expressly recognize a constitutional privilege to file complaints against police officers, are particularly disturbing because the privilege is seen by the courts as an absolute privilege, meaning that the officer cannot bring a civil action against the complainant *even if the complaint was made with knowledge that the complaint was false.* This privilege therefore far exceeds even the qualified privilege of the *New York Times* case (above), which can be defeated by a showing that the defendant knew that the statements were false.

Because of the circumstances of the *Stern* case (above), the exact scope of the decision is not yet clear, but its implications are grave. General application of the principles there discussed would in effect totally prohibit any police officer from suing for any complaint made against the officer, regardless of how unfounded or malicious the complaint might be. (This result would please many segments of our society. See below.)

The courts have long recognized a media privilege to publish anything "newsworthy," a privilege which may defeat either defamation or right of privacy actions.[7] Furthermore, where a police supervisor or other municipal official is the defendant, the official may enjoy a common-law qualified or absolute privilege for the statements made or actions taken.[8] These matters are also discussed in Chapter 8.

195

c. Limited Duty.

The premises owner may have no duty to the officer to keep the premises in good repair; where no such duty exists, the officer injured by a premises defect cannot recover for the injury. This defense therefore confronts the officer who brings suit for premises injuries in jurisdictions which hold police officers to be "licensees" or the equivalent. Fortunately, we may be witnessing a trend away from such restrictive holdings. The licensee rule is discussed in full detail in Chapter 5.

d. Provocation and Related Defenses.

In many suits, primarily those for intentional torts such as battery, the defense will be that the officer in some manner provoked the attack. If it can be shown that the officer did in fact provoke the defendant, or otherwise give the defendant justification for assaulting the officer, the chances of recovery will be greatly diminished. Thus, where the defendant can show that the officer failed to identify himself, or used excessive force, or even behaved in a rude and threatening manner to the defendant, it may give support to a self-defense plea, or, at the least, cause the plaintiff officer to lose the sympathy of the jury — both fatal to the officer's cause of action. Moreover, in some jurisdictions there is a right to resist unlawful arrest, which may cause the plaintiff officer to lose the case if the officer acted without authority or exceeded his authority.[9]

2. *Limits Imposed upon Police Plaintiff Suits by Statute*

In some jurisdictions, at least, the officer's right to be a plaintiff may be affected by statute. This is often the case with workmen's compensation laws, particularly where the officer has accepted benefits from the employer or from the employer's insurance company for the injury. Rights of subrogation or other limitations may seriously modify the

196

officer's prospects as a potential plaintiff, and this point should be checked carefully before accepting benefits or bringing suit.[10]

3. Countersuits and Administrative Action

While the entire purpose of this book has been to make officers aware of their rights under law and to encourage them to assert these rights, a warning is in order. *Before any civil action is attempted, the plaintiff officer should consult counsel and determine if there is a sound legal basis for the bringing of a civil action.* Unless there is some reasonable basis to believe that the officer does indeed have a right of action, the officer may, by bringing the action, be exposed to a retaliatory countersuit. While it has been held that an officer does not violate a defendant's civil rights by bringing a civil action against him,[11] the officer may be liable under common-law tort principles, *e.g.,* for malicious prosecution, if the officer's suit is unfounded and ultimately fails. Therefore, *use the system, but do not abuse it.* The police officer has no more right to bring an unfounded civil suit than the defendants discussed in this book. Furthermore, the bringing of a lawsuit may contravene departmental regulations, resulting in disciplinary action. Suits filed against departmental supervisors are particularly likely to lead to administrative sanctions, which may be upheld by the courts.[12]

B. PRACTICAL OBSTACLES

In addition to the numerous and formidable legal obstacles facing the plaintiff police officer, certain difficulties of a practical nature must be overcome as well. Among these are the difficulty of obtaining legal representation, the difficulty of enforcing a judgment, and the less tangible but perhaps equally powerful deterrent posed by the considerable opposition which exists to the entire concept of the police plaintiff suit.

197

1. *Obtaining Legal Counsel*

The problem of obtaining legal counsel has already been discussed in Chapter 2. As there noted, it is difficult to locate competent, experienced attorneys who will accept police plaintiff cases. Many attorneys avoid such cases because of antipathy toward law enforcement officers generally; others because they do not foresee sufficient financial reward. (See below.) Nevertheless, most urban areas will have one or more attorneys who specialize in representing police officers, and these attorneys are usually easily located by word-of-mouth or through police associations. This book includes acknowledgements of the help received by the author in the preparation of this book from attorneys in various parts of the country who are involved with civil litigation by police officers. There are, of course, many other attorneys in government and in private practice who engage in counseling and representing law enforcement personnel.

2. *Enforcement of Judgments*

As noted in several earlier portions of this work, the difficulty of obtaining a judgment is often not as formidable as the difficulty of enforcing it when it is obtained. Both officer and attorney contemplating the prospect of trying to collect damages from an indigent defendant may come to the conclusion that it is simply not worth proceeding because of the unlikelihood of actually obtaining payment of a judgment even if one should be obtained in court.

This concern is evident in public comments made by attorneys about police plaintiff cases. For example, *The Washington Post* quoted one attorney who had just won a $150,000 judgment from a defendant who was unable to pay it, as saying: "Lawyers tend to shy away from these kind[s] of cases . . . because you are not going to pay your bills with them." [13] Another lawyer was quoted as follows:

How's a lawyer going to get paid? . . . What good does it do to get a $150,000 verdict from a man who

198

can't pay? An awful lot of judges' time, court time and legal time goes down the drain running after a pot at the end of a rainbow. I don't think it's worth it.[14]

As noted earlier, while this concern is both real and proper, it has perhaps too often in the past been allowed to dissuade officers from bringing suits. Chapter 3 discusses in detail a number of defendants, other than the actual assailant, who may be financially responsible for the injury, including:

a. Other participants, co-conspirators, groups and organizations;

b. Employers;

c. Custodians;

d. Premises owners;

e. Insurance companies;

f. Vendors, donors, etc., of dangerous instruments; and

g. Governmental bodies and officers.

In addition, the possibility should not be overlooked that the individual assailant who appears to be judgment-proof may in fact have reachable assets or may acquire them in the near future. The fact that a potential defendant *says* that he is indigent does not necessarily mean that he really *is* indigent, as anyone who has been involved with the criminal law process well knows. Possible methods of collecting a judgment might include:

a. Discovery procedures, usually established by statute, to determine a judgment debtor's actual assets by questioning under oath under penalties of perjury;

b. Private investigation to locate assets which have been hidden or denied by the defendant;

c. Execution upon personal property or proceedings to subject real estate to the lien of the judgment;

d. Garnishment of the judgment debtor's wages (if any).

Furthermore, the fact that there are no present assets which are subject to any of these modes of access should not necessarily deter potential plaintiffs, because the defendant, although impecunious at this point in time, may subsequently acquire assets — and judgments are normally effective and collectable for long periods, *e.g.,* twenty to forty years. Thus, for example, the minor who assaults a police officer, though presently without a penny, may reasonably be expected to improve his financial position over a period of time after his majority — especially if he happens to have a trust fund or an elderly or infirm rich uncle. Even lacking this happy chance, the defendant will presumably begin to generate income at some point — hopefully by legal means — which can be reached to satisfy the judgment.[15]

Bonds posted by the defendant may be another potential source of judgment satisfaction. In civil trials, there is normally a requirement that any party appealing a lower court decision post a bond to cover the costs of the appeal. If the appealing party is a defendant against whom a money judgment has been rendered in the trial court, the bond may, depending upon local procedure and the specific terms of the bond, cover payment of the judgment if the defendant-appellant is unsuccessful on appeal. In some instances, then, the plaintiff may be able to proceed against the bond itself or against the sureties on the bond.[16]

Criminal bonds are not normally available to satisfy civil judgments, although one abortive attempt to utilize a criminal bond in part payment of an officer's judgment has been reported.[17]

All of these possibilities should be considered and investigated before a right of action is abandoned for lack of economic potential. And, of course, in many instances the officer will be interested, in part at least, in obtaining personal vindication or in setting an example rather than in collecting any specific amount of money.

3. *External and Internal Opposition*

Los Angeles attorney George Franscell, counsel for the Los Angeles Police Protective League, recently observed: "When we first brought civil cases against people for attacking officers, they were shocked .... They said, you can't do that. You're policemen. You have no rights." [18]

The public attitude to which Mr. Franscell was referring is widespread. Many segments of our society are opposed to the entire concept of civil suits by police officers, and would limit or deny the officer's right to be a plaintiff.

The reasons behind this attitude vary from an unreasoning, knee-jerk hatred of the police in some quarters to a sincere conviction held by many persons that civil suits by law enforcement personnel have a "chilling effect" on the exercise of the citizen's "right to complain" to the authorities of police misconduct.

These views are *not* limited to militant radicals. Opposition to the police civil suit is evident in many strata of our social and legal hierarchy, ranging from left-wing "rights" groups to police officials themselves. For example:

1. In Memphis, three officers countersued two citizens who had filed charges against the officers with the Memphis Police Department's internal affairs office. The citizens' attorney reportedly was "notably upset" by this development, and was quoted as stating:

... the greatest effect the (officers') complaint will have is frightening citizens of the inner city from coming to the office of internal affairs with legitimate complaints for fear of being sued ....[19]

2. In St. Louis, an arrestee complained to the Police Inspector's Office that the three officers who arrested him had abused him physically and verbally. The Board

of Police Commissioners found the charges to be unsupported, and the officers sued the arrestee. The President of the Board of Police Commissioners reportedly publicly criticized the filing of the officers' suit, charging that it undermined the city's new citizen complaint procedure.[20]

3. In Los Angeles, four officers, in conjunction with the Los Angeles Police Protective Association, filed a $600,000 defamation action against a California resident who had charged the officers with brutality and false imprisonment. The judge reportedly dismissed the suit on the grounds that, as argued by defendant's counsel, "Any citizen who merely chooses to exercise the fundamental right of redress of grievances must be free to do so without the threat of civil liability." [21]

4. In Baltimore, the Baltimore Police Department's Personnel Service Board recommended that the department press *criminal* charges against citizens who make false complaints against officers. The top departmental officials rejected the proposal, observing (in remarks apparently embracing both civil and criminal proceedings) that the department cannot maintain the public's confidence unless it permits "a free flow of information from the public which it serves, without fear of retribution in the form of countersuits by the agency." [22]

Groups representing minorities and civil rights groups generally have been particularly vehement in their opposition. *Newsweek* magazine quoted an official of the American Civil Liberties Union (ACLU) on the subject of police plaintiff suits: "It is an organized effort to harass the citizenry whenever it speaks out against police wrongdoing." [23]

The ACLU official reportedly views suits by police officers against citizens as "an attempt to blame the victim." [24]

While major news media reporting of the trend toward civil suits by police officers has in general been objective, hints of disapproval creep in. One article concludes with the following: "To many citizens, policemen already have the upper hand in almost any encounter, from the pistols they carry to their credibility in court. The civil suit has added a new weapon to their arsenal." [25]

While the opposition to police suits has many motives, takes many forms, and comes from many sources, certain common factors are worth noting:

1. The primary objection is to suits by officers for alleged false complaints.

2. The primary concern is that such suits will deter citizens from making *legitimate* reports of police misconduct.

3. It is feared that this deterrent effect will have its greatest impact on minority groups, who, in the view of the critics of civil suits by police, most often have legitimate complaints to make.

The proponents of police plaintiff suits, on the other hand, view such litigation as a deterrent to *false* complaints and, hopefully, *physical attacks* on officers.[26]

Whatever the rights or wrongs of these various views may be, the law enforcement profession cannot afford to disregard the arguments of those opposed to police plaintiff suits. Most especially, police associations and other potential plaintiffs must take care that the suits that are filed are factually and legally justified. The filing of questionable actions will only add fuel to the arguments of those who would like very much to deny police officers access to the civil courts. The fact that the plaintiff officer has been the victim of physical or verbal assault is regarded by many opponents as totally irrelevant; as one ACLU official has reportedly put it, "victims don't have rights." [27]

203

CHAPTER 10 — NOTES

1. *See* Fancil v. Q.S.E. Foods, Inc., 60 Ill. 2d 552, 328 N.E.2d 538 (1975) (danger was "obvious" and "inherent in their (the officers') occupations").

2. *Cf.* Burgard v. Eff, 1 Ohio App. 2d 483, 30 Ohio Op. 2d 503, 205 N.E.2d 400 (1965).

3. 376 U.S. 254, 84 S. Ct. 710, 11 L. Ed. 2d 686 (1964).

4. *See* Ch. 8 *supra* for citations.

5. *See, e.g.,* Imig v. Ferrar, 70 Cal. App. 3d 48, 138 Cal. Rptr. 540 (1977) (absolute privilege for statements made in departmental investigation of police officer); and THE POLICE PLAINTIFF, 76-2, at 7 ("fundamental right of redress of grievances," libel action by police officers dismissed). *See also* Wainman v. Bowler, 576 P.2d 268, 271 (Mont. 1978) ("freedom to speak foolishly and without moderation").

6. Stern v. United States Gypsum Inc., 547 F.2d 1329 (7th Cir.), *cert. denied,* 434 U.S. 975, 98 S. Ct. 533, 54 L. Ed. 2d 467 (1977).

7. *See* McNutt v. New Mexico State Tribune Co., 88 N.M. 162, 538 P.2d 804 (N.M. App. 1975), *cert. denied,* 540 P.2d 248 (1975).

8. *See, e.g.,* Hanzimanolis v. City of New York, 88 Misc. 2d 681, 388 N.Y.S.2d 826 (1976) (memo of deputy police commissioner absolutely privileged). This immunity does not extend to public defenders, however. Barto v. Felix, 378 A.2d 927 (Pa. Sup. 1977). *See also* Harris v. Harvey, 419 F. Supp. 30 (E.D. Wis. 1976) (racial slurs by judge, Civil Rights Act suit by police lieutenant stated a cause of action); Ramacciotti v. Zinn, 550 S.W.2d 217 (Mo. App. 1977) (police chief's statements not absolutely privileged). For a general discussion of immunity in a police plaintiff case, *see* Meester v. Davies, 11 Cal. App. 3d 342, 89 Cal. Rptr. 711 (1970).

9. *See* White v. Morris, 345 So.2d 461 (La. 1977) (right to resist unlawful arrest).

10. *See* Chs. 1, 3 *supra*.

11. Symkowski v. Miller, 294 F. Supp. 1214 (E.D. Wis. 1969).

12. *See* Norton v. City of Santa Ana, 15 Cal. App. 3d 419, 93 Cal. Rptr. 37 (1971) (police lieutenant filed defamation suit against chief and others; was subsequently fired).

13. Washington Post, Feb. 5, 1978, at A6, quoting attorney William E. Artz.

14. Washington Post, Feb. 5, 1978, at A6, quoting the attorney for the U.S. Park Police union.

15. *The Police Plaintiff,* reporting a case in which an Arlington, Va. police sergeant recovered a large judgment from a defendant who had shot the officer in the back of the head execution-style, noted that: "Although Sergeant Dreischer's chances of recovering his judgment or even a part

205

of it are slight, his attorney, William E. Artz, pointed out that the judgment lasts for 20 years and 'there may be a time when Turner will have some assets.' " (THE POLICE PLAINTIFF, 76-3, at 3.) The defendant, who was also sentenced to 40 years in the penitentiary for armed robbery and malicious wounding, "will become eligible for parole in 10 years." (*Id.*) *See also* Washington Post, Sun., Feb. 5, 1978, at A6, in which Mr. Artz was quoted as having pointed out the possibility that Dreischer may inherit money sometime during the judgment's 20-year life. Mr. Artz noted that, when apprehended, Dreischer was driving a Lincoln Continental belonging to his father.

16. *See* 5 AM. JUR. 2d *Appeal and Error* § 1029 *et seq.* (1962).

17. *The Police Plaintiff* reported the case of Knox v. Pannell, Circuit Ct., Cook County, Ill. (1976), in which an officer was suing an assailant who had posted a $10,000 bond on a related criminal charge. Following a judgment for the plaintiff officer, the circuit court judge ordered a portion of the criminal bond (which had meanwhile been forfeited) be turned over to the plaintiff as part payment of the civil judgment. The county officials refused to comply, and another judge overturned the order. THE POLICE PLAINTIFF, 76-2, at 3, and 78-2, at 3.

18. Quoted in THE BLUE LINE, Vol. 32, No. 9, at 3 (Aug. 1978).

19. THE POLICE PLAINTIFF, 77-3, at 8.

20. THE POLICE PLAINTIFF, 76-1, at 5.

21. THE POLICE PLAINTIFF, 76-2, at 7.

22. THE POLICE PLAINTIFF, 76-3, at 5.

23. NEWSWEEK, March 6, 1978.

24. *Id.*

25. *Id.*

26. *See* Ch. 1 *supra.*

27. Attributed to an official of the Maryland American Civil Liberties Union by the Washington Star-News, July 19, 1975, at 1, quoted in Carrington, *Victims' Rights Litigation,* 11 U. RICH. L. REV. 447 (Spring 1977).

Chapter 11

TACTICAL CONSIDERATIONS

This chapter discusses briefly some of the tactical aspects of police plaintiff litigation. The points covered here have been derived from a study of the reported cases and from discussions and correspondence with attorneys who handle police litigation. In examining this material, the reader should keep several points in mind:

1. These are *observations and suggestions only.* They are *not* rules or universal principles.

2. Even if they may be regarded as rules, they are at best very *general* rules. They may not be applicable, or of any importance, in a particular litigation.

3. Even where they are applicable, counsel may quite properly decide, under the peculiar circumstances of the individual case, to ignore them.

Nevertheless, these are matters which figure in and affect most police plaintiff litigation, and they should be considered carefully before being ignored or rejected in a specific case.

A. MULTIPLE ACTIONS

1. *Multiple Causes of Action*

Many factual situations will give rise to more than one cause of action. For example, it has already been pointed out that such torts as assault, battery, false imprisonment, and defamation frequently all result from one incident, and damages may be obtained for each of them individually. Unless local procedure dictates otherwise, or counsel considers it tactically inadvisable, the officer should bring as many tort actions as he has causes of action. These may be joined in the same complaint (and usually are), but there is normally no necessity to elect between tort remedies or to abandon one because another has been specified in the complaint. As noted, however, tactical considerations may make it advisable to omit one or more counts. For example, counsel may wish to avoid the appearance of "piling it on" the defendant, which might cause the plaintiff to lose the sympathy of the jury; or counsel may prefer not to assert a questionable claim for fear of weakening the overall case and jeopardizing the chances of recovery on other claims for which liability is clear.

2. *Multiple Plaintiffs*

If more than one person has a cause of action, it may be desirable for all plaintiffs to bring suits. For example, if an invasion of privacy has affected the officer's family as well as the officer, each member of the family is entitled to sue, and usually should, in order to maximize the total recovery.

Where a number of *officers* have been injured, all of course have the right to sue. But it may or may not be advisable for all to sue *in the same action.* While there are no hard statistics to prove or disprove the theory, it appears that *increasing the number of officers who are plaintiffs in the case decreases the chances of a successful recovery.* There are notable exceptions to this, of course, especially at the trial level,[1] but in general it seems that whenever it appears to the court or the jury that a large number of officers are "ganging up" on one defendant, or that the case has, in effect, become a class action, whose result will establish precedent for recoveries by an entire department or for numerous other members of the law enforcement profession, there is a tendency to try to find an excuse for avoiding a holding favorable to the plaintiff officers.

Although these considerations are present in any multiple-plaintiff case, the problems are aggravated in police plaintiff cases by the anti-police bias of our society. Where one injured officer would receive sympathy, ten may arouse hostility, because they are perceived not as individual human beings but as "the" police.

This phenomenon is also apparent when police associations appear as named plaintiffs. In such cases, courts may be more reluctant to find in favor of the officers because the result will usually be not just compensation for one injured person, but a precedent-setting decision which will affect many future cases—a result which the courts seem to prefer to avoid.

Persons other than the injured officer who may be able to maintain actions as named plaintiffs are discussed in Chapter 3.

B. NEGLIGENCE VERSUS INTENTIONAL TORT ACTIONS

The same set of facts may give the officer the option of suing for either negligence or an intentional tort. Here, it may be necessary under local procedure to elect between them and to sue for either one or the other.

Generalizing broadly, intentional torts are usually easier to prove, and punitive damages are almost always available. The victim of an intentional tort may be viewed more sympathetically by the jury, and the defenses of contributory negligence and assumption of the risk are avoided.

In some instances, however, counsel may prefer to proceed on a negligence theory because that route offers better access to the deep pocket of a third party, or counsel may feel that the negligence approach offers a better potential dollar recovery in a specific jurisdiction or case. In many instances, for example, the defendant's insurance company will be obligated to pay if the defendant was negligent, but not if the tort was intentional.[2]

Many states permit pleading in the alternative; in such jurisdictions, the plaintiff may allege that the injury was caused *either* by negligence or by intent. This is desirable in cases in which the plaintiff is uncertain as to what the defendant's state of mind was or what the proof may show.[3]

Attorneys experienced in police plaintiff cases emphasize the desirability of suing for *both* negligence and intent in many instances. Mr. George Franscell, attorney for the Los Angeles Police Protective League, points out that even in a case which appears to be a classic intentional tort, adding a count in negligence may be advantageous where the defendant has some type of liability insurance coverage. The insurance company will then be obligated to defend the suit and, if the defendant is found negligent, to pay the judgment. For this reason, both the plaintiff *and the defendant* may be eager to find some basis for a verdict of negligence, with obvious resulting benefits to the plaintiff.[4]

In addition, of course, suing on two counts makes it possible for the plaintiff to recover on one theory even if the other fails. Consequently, it may be desirable to sue for both intent and negligence even in cases in which insurance is not involved.

C. COUNTERCLAIMS

It seems to be generally agreed that a police officer who becomes a *defendant* is often wise to take the offensive and file a counterclaim in the action, thereby becoming a plaintiff as well as a defendant.[5] A study done by Jury Verdict Research, Inc., revealed that while defendants are exonerated in only 35 percent of all jury cases, defendants who counterclaimed in the action obtained favorable verdicts in 68 percent of the suits in which counterclaims were filed. Furthermore, in 48 percent of the cases in which favorable verdicts were obtained by counterclaiming defendants, the defendant not only avoided payment of damages *to* the plaintiff, but was actually awarded damages *from* the plaintiff who had orginally brought the suit.[6] There is also reason to believe that the counterclaim reduces the damages awarded to the plaintiff even in those actions in which the plaintiff actually prevails.[7]

The best defense, it appears, is still the attack.[8]

D. SETTLEMENT VERSUS TRIAL

In many civil suits, the case does not go to trial but is settled by the parties prior to the trial date. Cases are typically settled for figures far short of the amount demanded in the complaint, and, because the settlement is in effect a compromise, are usually for less than might have been expected in a successful trial. (While the sample is too small to be statistically reliable, figures compiled from cases in the author's files indicate that for cases of all types, the average police officer plaintiff's verdict is about 7½ times greater than the average settlement.)

This does *not* mean that every case should be brought to trial; on the contrary, the difficulty of obtaining a favorable verdict at trial is what makes settlements attractive in many police plaintiff cases. It is often far better to accept a small settlement than to risk the uncertainties of a trial, especially since the settlement usually provides the officer with the public vindication or satisfaction in principle so often sought by police plaintiffs.

Thus, the amount offered in settlement must be balanced against the risk that the trial will produce a defendant's verdict — *i.e.,* nothing — and this risk varies according to the type of tort action being brought. As noted elsewhere in this book, it is very difficult for police officers to prevail in defamation actions; it is relatively easier in negligence actions for personal injuries; and perhaps the highest percentage of success is experienced in actions for the intentional torts, especially battery.

No set of statistics can be allowed to sway the final decision in a particular case, however; the decision to settle or not to settle must always be made in light of the particular circumstances in the specific case, and while it is technically the client's decision to accept or not to accept a settlement offer, the plaintiff officer should rely heavily upon counsel's analysis of the situation before making the decision.

E. LOCAL CONDITIONS AND ATTITUDES

The local situation will have a powerful influence on most police plaintiff cases, including a decision as to whether to seek or accept a settlement offer. While many factors may be involved, the following elements may be worthy of consideration:

1. *Attitude Toward Law Enforcement in the Community Generally*

Different localities view law enforcement differently. Thus, different sections of the country have different attitudes toward the police, and there is considerable evidence that the urban environment often breeds more hostility toward law enforcement than the small town or rural area. These attitudes may be reflected in the makeup and response of the jury.

2. *Type of Case*

The nature of the case itself gives some clue as to the officer's chances of success. For example, was the police officer the only one injured, or was the defendant also hurt? [9] Also potentially difficult are cases in which the defendant is a member of a minority racial or ethnic group. Such cases tend to arouse emotions in the community and to attract rights groups and others to the defense. This is an especially difficult situation for the officer in cases in which the defendant has charged the officer with brutality or racial or ethnic slurs.

212

3. *Attitude of the Courts*

No evaluation of the chances of success can be complete until consideration has been given to the attitudes of the trial judge who will preside over the case and of the appellate court or courts which will pass upon the propriety of the plaintiff's verdict if one is actually obtained. Local court judges in particular vary a great deal in their attitudes toward police suits, and a trial judge who wishes to do so can terminate a case very quickly, regardless of the facts or the law. Counsel will therefore include this factor in both the evaluation and the strategic and tactical planning of the case.

As noted at the beginning of this section, the foregoing points are suggestions and observations only; they are not rules, or, if they are, they should frequently be broken.

Again, the value of competent, experienced counsel becomes obvious, for the factors discussed here are just a fraction of the multitude of judgments and decisions, whether logical or intuitive, which must be made in the course of litigation.

For the police officer, being a plaintiff is itself sometimes difficult; being a *successful* plaintiff is even more difficult. And, as opposition to the officer's right to sue grows and consolidates, it will become even more difficult than it is now.

Nevertheless, more and more officers are seeking redress in the civil courts, and they will continue to do so.

As noted earlier, this trend has been forced upon the police by the increasing risks of their profession; risks vastly increased by the anti-police bias of our present society. The police are, indeed, tired of being targets and punching bags; but firearms and nightsticks and mace cannot protect them against the hostility being manifested today.

Perhaps the civil suit will indeed prove to be the most effective weapon in the law enforcement officer's defensive arsenal.

CHAPTER 11— NOTES

1. Many multiple-officer plaintiff cases are successful at the trial level but are struck down by appellate courts. An example is Meiners v. Moriarity, 563 F.2d 343 (7th Cir. 1977), in which eight officers received a verdict of $120,000 in a trial court, only to have the award set aside by the Court of Appeals.

2. *See, e.g.,* Passman v. Bienvenu, 277 So.2d 451 (La. App. 1973).

3. *Id. See also* THE POLICE PLAINTIFF, 77-2, at 6 (defendant "negligently or intentionally" stamped on officer's toe).

4. A legitimate claim of negligence may be made in many instances where the injury appears on the face of it to be an intentional one. For example, in many instances the defendant attacks a police officer while intoxicated by alcohol or other drugs. Although this appears at first glance to be an "intentional" tort — battery — it may also be argued that the defendant's negligence in allowing himself to become intoxicated has caused the defendant to lose control of himself and attack the officer — thereby permitting a recovery in negligence.

5. All sources consulted appear to agree that the counterclaim is a desirable tactical response to a lawsuit against the officer, at least when the officer has suffered some actual, serious injury. One attorney experienced in the defense of police cases indicated that he would not normally counterclaim where the officer defendant has suffered only minor injuries, such as superficial bumps and bruises.

6. Jury Verdict Research, Inc., *Cross Complaints* (1977). *See, e.g.,* Geisler v. Bianco, No. 74-C-2671 (N.D. Ill. 1976), in which an officer was sued under 42 U.S.C. § 1983 for use of excessive force. Attorney Frederic B. Weinstein, then Assistant State's Attorney for Cook County, who was defending Officer Bianco, counterclaimed for injuries (loss of teeth) sustained by the officer during the arrest. The jury rejected the arrestee's claims against the officer and awarded the officer $2,500 in damages on the counterclaim. The case is reported in THE POLICE PLAINTIFF, 76-2, 3, and 77-4, at 12. (Some details were provided directly to the author by Mr. Weinstein.)

7. Because of the mystery surrounding the deliberative process of juries, this is mere speculation, but it seems to be supported by logic and experience.

8. *See also* the feature articles in THE POLICE PLAINTIFF, 77-4, at 10, and 78-1, at 9, discussing counterclaims as a strategic and tactical device.

9. Consider, for example, the difficulty of the officer plaintiff who shoots and kills his assailant and then brings suit against the deceased assailant's estate. A strong case will be needed to prevail against the widow and children of the deceased assailant.

Index

A

FIREARMS.
Sales.
  Sale to unfit persons basis for liability to officer, pp. 66, 67.

H

HARRASSMENT.
Actions by family of the officer, p. 133.
Defenses.
  Consent, pp. 193, 194.
Intentional infliction of mental distress.
  Continued harrassment actionable, p. 133.
Not actionable by officer himself.
  Exceptions, p. 133.

I

IMPRISONMENT.
False imprisonment.
  See FALSE IMPRISONMENT.

INFLICTION OF MENTAL DISTRESS.
Actions by family of officer, p. 133.
Harassment.
  Continued harrassment actionable, p. 133.
Insults.
  Continuing course of insults.
    Actionable, p. 132.
Intentional infliction, pp. 127 to 130.
  Actions by family of officer, p. 133.
  Defenses.
    Consent, pp. 193, 194.
  Flagrant conduct required, p. 128.
  Harrassment.
    Continued harrassment required, p. 133.
  Insults.
    Continuous insults required, p. 132.
  Intent required, pp. 128, 129.
  Physical injury.
    Not required, p. 128.
  Police plaintiffs.
    Reluctance of officers to take advantage of this action, pp. 129, 130.
  Severe distress required, p. 128.
  Specific intent, pp. 128, 129.
  Threats.
    Continued course required, p. 132.
Negligent infliction.
  Physical impact.
    Not required, p. 130.
  Physical injury.
    Required, p. 130.

P

R

REMEDIES.
Damages.
See DAMAGES.
Injunctions.
See INJUNCTIONS.

S

SALES.
Alcoholic beverages.
Basis of liability to officer, p. 67.
Explosives.
Sales to unfit persons basis for liability to officer, pp. 66, 67.
Firearms.
Sale to unfit persons basis for liability to officer, pp. 66, 67.
Weapons.
Sale to unfit persons basis for liability to officer, pp. 66, 67.
SETTLEMENTS.
Tactical considerations, pp. 211, 212.
SLANDER.
See DEFAMATION.
SOVEREIGN IMMUNITY.
Defense to suit against governmental entity, p. 68.
SUBROGATION.
Employer.
Contract, pp. 54, 55.
Equitable subrogation, pp. 55, 56.
Statute, p. 54.
Insurance companies, pp. 56, 57.
Police associations, p. 51.

T

TACTICAL CONSIDERATIONS.
Counterclaims.
Filing by police, pp. 210, 211.
Local conditions and attitudes.
Attitude of the courts, p. 213.
Attitude toward law enforcement, p. 212.
Type of case, p. 212.
Multiple actions, pp. 207, 208.
Multiple plaintiffs, pp. 208, 209.
Negligence versus intentional tort actions, pp. 209, 210.
Settlements versus trial, pp. 211, 212.